PANDORA'S BOX?

PANDORA'S BOX?
Companion Papers on Motivation, Access and the Media

Commissioned by the Further Education Funding Council for its Widening Participation Committee

Naomi Sargant and Alan Tuckett

Published by the National Institute of Adult Continuing Education
(England and Wales)
21 De Montfort Street, Leicester, LE1 7GE
Company registration no. 2603322
Charity registration no. 1002775
The NIACE website is http://www.niace.org.uk

First published 1997

CATALOGUING IN PUBLICATION DATA
A CIP record for this title is available from the British Library
ISBN 1 86201 034 X

Typeset by Midlands Book Typesetters
Cover design by Boldface
Printed in Great Britain by Russell Press

Contents

Naomi Sargant is a Senior Research Fellow of NIACE, a visiting professor at the Open University, where she was Pro-Vice Chancellor, before joining Channel 4 as founding Senior Commissioning Editor for educational programming. She convenes a task group of the National Advisory Group for Continuing Education and Lifelong Learning on New Technologies, and advises the European Union on the SOCRATES programme.

Alan Tuckett has been Director of NIACE since 1988 after working in Brighton and in the Inner London Education Authority. He is Vice-Chair of the National Advisory Group for Continuing Education and Lifelong Learning, and convenes its Finance and Funding task group. He is a Special Professor in Continuing Education at the University of Nottingham, and was awarded the OBE in 1995.

Introduction

The two papers included in this volume were commissioned from the National Institute of Adult Continuing Education by the Further Education Funding Council, as contributions to the work of its Widening Participation Committee, chaired by Helena Kennedy QC.

NIACE welcomed the establishment of the Committee; was pleased when the Chair of the NIACE Executive Committee, Judith Summers, was asked to join it and chair one of its sub-groups; and has warmly welcomed Helena Kennedy's vision in *Learning Works*, and the Committee's main recommendations.

The papers that make up *Pandora's Box?* were commissioned in January and submitted in March 1997. They are published by NIACE, with the encouragement and support of the FEFC.

In presenting these two papers NIACE made seven recommendations for the Committee to consider, which are listed on pages 66 and 67. These were broadly endorsed by the Widening Participation Committee. Its recommendations on stimulating the demand for learning were clear and welcome:

The government should:

- in creating the 'University for Industry', draw upon the expertise of the Council, further education providers and other key organisations, to develop a service which will meet the needs of the widest spectrum of learners, and support the 'New Learning Pathway'
- legislate to make it a duty for all terrestrial television channels to educate as well as to entertain and inform
- work with the BBC and independent broadcasters to explore the possibility of dedicated television channels to support learning
- take steps, in partnership with key national players, to create a mass demand for learning which includes the whole spectrum of the population
- develop a comprehensive 'Charter for Learning', which should be promoted through a national publicity campaign and logo
- make it a key role of the local strategic partnerships to promote clear and consistent messages about the value of learning and the range of opportunities available, and to collaborate with the 'University for Industry' at local level
- develop the role of the Employment Service in promoting the value of, and the opportunities for, learning, particularly to those with little recent experience of learning or who lack basic skills and qualifications.

The Council should:

- recognise in its aims that it has responsibility to work with others to encourage and promote demand for learning
- welcome and promote the potential new role for the further education sector created by the 'University for Industry'.

Motivation, Access and the Media[1]

1 Choices and structures

1.1 Choosing to use the media for adult learning

Developments in media technology are affecting education at every level. Most of the technologies that will help learning and teaching into the next century already exist. They are available to industry and education and training institutions, but they are not yet all accessible to learners at home, although they will be soon. They have different costs, and different benefits. The challenge is to harness the most appropriate technology to our purpose. If we fail to do this the technology or its owners, through the market, will manage us rather than we, the education and training community, manage it for learners and our needs and purposes.

The convergence of television and telecommunications means that the television set of the future will also be a telecomputer providing interactivity, and the ability to link into a wide variety of channels, networks and databases. The television set can already be used to deliver broadcasting, narrowcasting, video, cable and satellite. Whether the message comes through to the screen from a terrestrial transmitter, a video, from satellite direct, via cable or via phone lines and a computer will simply not matter to people at home. What matters will be accessibility, choice, quality and price. The term Internet is becoming, misleadingly, almost a synonym or metaphor for these changes, but it is in reality only a small part of them.

We choose to use the media for education and training if we can reach more people than we could using conventional ways, or if we can teach them better, more effectively or more cheaply, or if we can reach people we otherwise could not reach. In particular we are interested in bringing new people into learning and in increasing participation. This paper is therefore less concerned with curricular and content issues than with issues of access and motivation. It is also concerned with how learning is offered as issues such as the delivery of learning, the flexibility of provision and other structural issues affect access and motivation.

For broadcasters, as for educators, this divides into two parts: access for those who know what they want, most of whom are already into the educational system; and access for those who may not yet know what they would want if the opportunities were appropriate and appropriately offered. In parenthesis, we note that the first category divides into those who know what they want and *will seek it* out themselves and those who are still in a *subject* condition where decisions about learning resources are mainly taken for learners by teachers or trainers.

1.2 Broadcasting and access – as the reference case

It is helpful to look first at broadcasting as the reference case since broadcasting is the most accessible of the communications media: virtually everyone has a television set and the signal is universal. The strength of broadcast TV is that it reaches everywhere and is free at the point

[1] In preparing this paper for the FEFC, the author has drawn on and extended a number of her own chapters, articles and speeches, both published and unpublished. The main ones drawn on are not individually referenced each time, but are marked * in the References.

of use. It reduces at a stroke two of the three main barriers to access faced by all other forms of education: geography and finance.

Broadcast education for adults is not just important for transmitting curriculum-based programmes. It plays a particularly strong role in raising awareness, stimulating demand and offering follow-up resources to programming. Five main functions had been identified by ACACE (1982) for broadcasting, which have recently been reaffirmed as important by Groombridge (1996).

These functions are:

1. Providing educative programmes which are educative in themselves.
2. Programmes, in principle from any part of the output, whose educational value is enhanced by publications (sometimes major texts in their own right).
3. Programmes that spread awareness of adult education, publicise learning opportunities, encourage the use of locally available facilities.
4. Programme and other materials, used as resources by tutors in face-to-face settings, a service much facilitated by appropriate off-air recording and copyright arrangements.
5. Broadcast and recorded programmes as an element in an integrated teaching scheme – whether devoted to one subject, one issue or a complete curriculum.

A classic example of the first category was *The World at War*, which introduced many people to contemporary history, some of whom then enrolled with the OU. There are numerous examples of the second: Kenneth Clark's *Civilisation*, and David Bellamy's *Botanic Man* made by Thames are two such. *The Learning Zone* is now assisting proactively in the provision of the fourth category and targeting much of it directly to FE colleges. The Open University is, of course the classic example of the fifth category, and makes the link across to the increasing use of open and distance learning, a topic to be returned to later in the paper. It is the third category that is most important for this discussion. Television in particular is extremely powerful in informing people about opportunities and therefore in making the opportunities more accessible.

The function of providing information about opportunities to people was extremely important at the start of the Open University, as it was nearly twenty years later to the Open College. A survey among the general public before the Open University went on air showed that one in three of the population knew about it, and of those, one in five knew that it was to use BBC television and radio. Two years on, in 1973, the proportion knowing of the Open University had increased to 44% with one in three knowing it used television and radio.

The Open College was launched in Autumn 1987 with its broadcasting on Channel Four. Research carried out in the summer of 1988 showed over a third of the population claiming to have heard of the Open College. More surprisingly, television was recorded as the source of that information for 73% of those who had heard of it.

More recently, Adult Learners' Week, involving a variety of styles of programming from across the broadcasting spectrum, has demonstrated the value of broadcasting in reaching out to large numbers of people interested in learning and stimulating them to telephone the helpline, enquire about local opportunities and enrol for courses. Details of the strategies and success of these campaigns appears in Alan Tuckett's parallel paper, *Motivation is Curriculum*.

The second basic point about access to *broad*casting is a simple one: that people who know what they want and are sufficiently motivated can be asked or persuaded to watch at less accessible times of day, ie, effectively through narrowcasting on broadcast TV. We already accept, for example, that some programming for 'closed' target groups, both on radio and TV, can be downloaded at night: radio for schools and TV training programmes for nurses. Much educational programming, including some for the OU, is already transmitted in anti-social hours and at night-time.

The educational access argument for keeping such narrowcasting as the Open University and *The Learning Zone* on broadcast TV, as it is the cheapest method of mass delivery to people in their own homes, is therefore a powerful one. While space remains available on broadcast channels, and included in this is the possibility that such space is protected by regulation, then clearly broadcasting is the most accessible option for both types of programming. Of course using downtime requires additionally the ownership of a video-recorder, but this is increasingly widespread in the UK.

The fifth category is also important to this discussion as the delivery of high quality learning resources to people free at the point of use is a vital part of improving access. The OU started its broadcasting before the widespread arrival of video-recorders and while its programmes were always transmitted at the edges of existing schedules, they were still accessible for motivated learners. Increasingly such programmes are not watched live, but are recorded on video.

1.3 Why do we choose to use the media?

Why should we move from the time-honoured system of face-to face teaching which has served society well for generations and which is still the preferred mode for teaching the intellectual elite? We now choose to use new and older media instead of conventional face-to-face teaching if:

- it is possible to reach more learners than through conventional face-to-face methods.
- learning can be offered more effectively or more flexibly. For example, a video can show a lab demonstration more clearly than it can be seen by 200 students in an over-crowded laboratory.
- different learners can be reached, for example, shift-workers, women at home, prisoners.
- using the media allows us to offer people access to knowledge and experiences: to music, culture, world experts, the knowledge of other countries that they otherwise could not personally experience.
- and with large enough numbers, it can be done cost-effectively.

A simple option, still widely used, is just to point a camera at a teacher and record what is normally taught in a class-room. But with the ability to choose to use different media for different purposes, what we need to do conceptually is to disaggregate the knowledge, skills and experience we have normally provided face-to-face in order to use different and more appropriate media to communicate different parts of it. Different media have different functions and bring different benefits. Film and video, for example, are particularly good at showing people things they normally cannot see, especially moving visual images.

Science at the Open University provides a good example of disaggregating or deconstructing the knowledge and skills which were heretofore provided through a teacher in a laboratory. All commentators had said that it was impossible to teach science at a distance. Part of the time typically spent in a university science laboratory is used for the teaching of theory, part for observation and part on practical work. Much of the observational component in OU courses is provided through TV and video, and the practical work through home experiment kits and summer schools. Radio brings lectures/interviews with well-known scientists and outside academics leaving the core of the theory and factual knowledge to the print component. The quality of the experience is thus enriched rather than diminished when these elements are reaggregated by the learner.

Using media is not necessarily a cheap option, though if the number of learners is large enough, it is likely to be. Educators such as the Open University who have access to broadcasting, for example, have an extremely valuable technology which enables them to deliver programmes to a larger number of people very cheaply. It is not that the programmes are necessarily cheap to make, but because the cost of programming and transmission is borne up front, and predicated on a very large number of viewers watching, the cost per person viewing, or programme delivered is usually very low and there is no cost to the viewer at the point of viewing. These issues will be returned to later.

Broadcasting is just one of many delivery systems and it is no longer sensible to talk about broadcasting as if it is somehow special and different from other delivery systems. Our existing broadcast channels already engage in narrowcasting part of the time for the OU, for BBC's *The Learning Zone*, and for Channel 4 schools programmes. All of these are increasingly making programmes which are designed, *ab initio*, to have both a broadcast and a video life. The same programmes are available for copying off-air for hire or on video or sometimes re-edited in a different structure for mediation by teachers. And, of course by reverse, films for the cinema and works made for other audiences find their way on to the television screen.

Television itself is about to change. Rupert Murdoch was ahead of the game in understanding the importance of these changes for education and for the leisure industry when he addressed the Edinburgh Television Festival in 1989:

> *The television set of the future will be in reality a telecomputer linked by fibre-optic cable to a global cornucopia of programmes and nearly infinite libraries of data, education and entertainment. All with full interactivity . . . These telecomputers will bring a huge variety of channels, including the ability to order up whatever you want to watch. It will revolutionise the way we are educated, the way we work and the way we relax.* (Murdoch,1989)

Nearly ten years on, with the imminent arrival of digital television, both satellite and terrestrial, as well as video on demand, the technology has arrived, though it has not yet reached colleges or people's homes at affordable prices. Even if teachers find Murdoch's future threatening it will certainly open up new opportunities for learners.

1.4 Terminology

The terms themselves, telematics, electronic education, multi-media, are not user-friendly. The OU, at its inception, was described as 'multi-media' just because it used a number of media in conjunction with each other. The term 'multi-media', now being used to encompass some of these new developments such as CD-Roms and audiographics, is taking on a new meaning and links together, as Rupert Murdoch indicated, the power of television with the power of the computer to which is increasingly added, new telecommunications facilities, hence telematics. Telematics is increasingly used to denote the convergence of television, computing and telecommunications.

The term 'electronic education', used by some in the UK, is not clear to many people and also smacks of 'education being provided for students' rather than a means of enabling learning. The use of the word 'learning' is preferred as it places the emphasis on the person who learns and avoids the unhelpful artificial distinction between education and training.

What matters, as we move to this great 'telecommunications highway' is that we determine how to use and manage these developments rather than allow the technology or the market to dictate how they are used. We need to be clear about what business we are in – what are we trying to offer to learners, what sort of people are we trying to reach, with what sort of content, through what sort of delivery systems and with what sort of resources available to help in this task?

1.5 Structural changes

New technologies have brought new choices, but they also impose some new limitations. We have tended to regard some structural changes in society as political when their cause is primarily technological. In the UK, for example, the BBC and ITV together held a monopoly of television broadcasting. Its breakdown was hastened by the arrival of Channel 4 in 1982 and the disaggregation of the component parts of what had previously been a 'vertically integrated' production and distribution system. However, the main cause has been the arrival of the new technologies of cable, satellite and video.

An eminent UK social scientist, Michael Young, in a speech to the Fabian Centenary School in 1984, used a series of evocative images to describe a set of related changes which had already taken place. He noted that there had already been a shift of scale of people's lives outside work.

> *The small (and private) has increasingly replaced the large (and public). The watch has replaced the public clock. The 'fridge has replaced the ice factory; the washing machine, the public laundry; the private bathroom, the municipal baths; the car, the bus or train; and TV, the cinema.* (Young,1984)

And even so, he suggested that the new home computer and teletext might replace the newspaper. What all these changes have to do with is accessibility, freedom and choice. It is obvious that the small (and private) are more accessible to the individuals and families that possess them than the large (and public). However, those who do not possess them are placed at an increasing disadvantage.

The provision of these services had developed into monopolies or near-monopolies of supply more because of their technological scale and nature than for any political or ideological reason. The 'community' as a whole paid for their provision, which was then available free to the citizen/user at the point of use. A benefit was that the provision was universally available, but the negative was that the structures did not allow much flexibility and individuality in use, particularly in relation to location.

An important characteristic was that such institutions tended to be producer- and production-led rather than user or market-led. Schools and universities have historically had just such a monopoly of supply and have been able to continue to be producer- and production-led rather than being led by the needs of the learners.

The same has been true of broadcasting. But with both of these we have taken for granted the principle of universality of access. What changes in the new technological and market-led scenario is that those who can afford the small and private maintain their access while those that cannot are increasingly denied it or may only be provided with a lower standard of service: the increase in car ownership has, for example, led to a reduction in public transport, whose users are now the ones with less money and less choice: the old, the young and the poor.

Behind this change lies the question of who pays and at what point in the process. The UK has traditionally taken a long-term view of the value of investment in the education of the young as an investment in the community and as feeding into public capital. And as with schooling, it has traditionally provided the further and higher levels of full-time initial education free at the point of use to the majority of learners and the cost has been paid by the community. This assumption is not carried over to lifelong learning, including adult education or indeed to part-time study, and is increasingly under pressure for full-time higher education with the means-testing of maintenance grants and the introduction of student loans. (Though it should be noted that the situation is now likely to change with the Dearing proposal to introduce tuition fees for higher education.)

Government has also increasingly been differentiating between education and training and between vocational and non-vocational education – a peculiar view to many in higher education who have been used to 'training' teachers and doctors as well 'educating' scholars, writers, researchers, etc. For most learners, the difference between education and training is not a relevant or helpful one. However, it is evident that the UK Government and indeed the European Union may wish to continue to differentiate between them. This affects policy developments and funding which in turn affects the provision of education and training. More government funding has been provided for vocational training than for general adult learning, and particular encouragement has been offered for the development of open and distance learning.

Education	Training
As an investment in the community	As a personal or private good
As feeding into public (ie, society's) capital	As feeding into private/employer's or personal capital
Working on longer time-scales	Shorter time-scales/requires quicker pay-off
Free at the point of use/paid for by the community	Paid for by individual/employer
Universality of provision	Selective provision
Public service	Private market
Provision through 'large and public'	Provision through 'small and private'
Large educational institutions with conventional (face-to-face) teaching	Open/distance learning available in flexible ways, in small units
Available in limited places	Available anywhere
Broadcasting – limited choice of channels	Narrow-casting and other media – video – cable/satellite – interactive video – pay channels – CD-ROM, CD-I etc
but free at point of use	but NOT free to the user

Figure 1: Education and training compared

Figure 1 identifies a number of characteristics which differentiate education and training and also relate to the structures of broadcasting and the newer media and to the distinctions made earlier. Historical structures of education and broadcasting are being changed by new technologies. The assumption that the community pays and services are free at the point of use is increasingly being replaced by the principle of user-pays.

The point, and it is a threatening one, is that just as new technologies have broken down the monopoly power of broadcasting, so the application of new media for open and distance learning is increasingly in a position to break down the monopoly of power of conventional educational institutions. For learners, it removes the barriers to access of time as well as of place. Open/distance learning can be delivered to or bought by people for use anywhere they wish. That is why it is so important in providing opportunities for adults, why open and distance learning have been encouraged by the Employment Department and embraced so readily by employers for training. The danger is that finance becomes the new barrier to access.

The reason for the extreme importance of broadcasting is that it has been able to deliver educational programming without financial and geographical barriers whether it is at the level of the Open University or the Open College or for family learning, for the unemployed, elderly, illiterate or handicapped groups. Such significant, and often large, groups will need to continue to be served by broadcasting. The function of opening people's eyes to new areas and stimulating the 'wantless' to pursue new learning also needs broadcasting, preferably on 'mass' channels, whether publicly or privately run. It is for this reason that adult educators argued for the 1996 Broadcasting Act to require some guaranteed educational provision on the new digital channels.

Providing these functions are protected and maintained on accessible terrestrial channels, it will also be important to add to the array of provision and to people's choice by using new technologies and new narrowcast options as effectively as possible.

1.6 The current spectrum of provision

Broadcasting itself offers a spectrum of opportunities which can be looked at as a continuum from mass broadcast to specialist narrowcast. The current range in the UK, prior to the arrival of new digital terrestrial and satellite channels, contains:

Broadcast:

- mass national eg, BBC1, networked ITV and Channel 5
- mass regional eg, ITV regions
- specialist national eg, BBC2 and Channel 4
- national radio
- local radio
  - BBC
  - commercial

Each of these can provide good time slots, adequate or grave-yard slots. Good slots are required for unmotivated audiences.

Narrow-cast:

- BBC *Learning Zone* (night-time down-loading for education and specialist audiences, usually recorded on video)
- local cable
- DBS satellite

All of these allow the delivery of programmes direct to people in their own homes. Some of them will be free and some will be charged for and encrypted. It is clear, for example, that the BBC's *Learning Zone* represents the extreme narrow-cast end of the BBC spectrum, but its advantage is that it is riding on the coat-tails of existing domestically available technology, does not require new investment at home and is clear-to-view. Apart from the cost of the decoder, simulcast channels from analogue broadcasters will remain free at the point of use. However, plans for many new digital and terrestrial satellite channels suggest many specialist channels for which there will be charges. Some new developments, such as video-on-demand, will also provide some interactivity.

1.7 Personalising and individualising broadcasting messages

The saving of resources with broadcasting as a technology comes from delivering one centrally produced message to large numbers of people. The message can be personalised in a number of ways. Options available for personalising messages include: face-to-face contact, post, phone, fax, telex, electronic mail/internet and audio-cassette. Personalising messages should not be confused with building in learner interactivity, a matter to be discussed later. The key point to remember is that the more a message is personalised or individualised the more it may cost!

1.8 Learning from the experience of the OU

The OU recently celebrated its 25th anniversary and has clearly demonstrated its success against such cynics who had described it initially as a 'pipedream'. A significant element in its early success, both in terms of credibility and accessibility, was its partnership with the BBC. It now has more than 200,000 students studying with it each year and over 130,000 have graduated since it began teaching in 1971, of whom one-third had less than the minimum entry requirements for entry to a conventional university. (Sargant,1996)

It is important to remember that what the Open University did was not just to make higher education much more accessible but to help people believe that it was accessible. Similar institutional projects to be discussed later have not yet been as successful at other educational levels.

Until the Open University was set up, just as broadcasting institutions such as the BBC had until recently a monopoly of broadcasting moving visual images, so universities had an effective monopoly of the provision of higher education. Originally provided to the elite on a one-to-one basis or for selected small groups, it was provided only in given locations and in predetermined ways, surrounded by rules and conventions which often had little to do with the nature of the learning to be achieved and a lot to do with maintaining closed professions and privilege. The OU opened the gate to the 'secret garden'. Perhaps its most important contribution has been to demystify knowledge and make it open and accessible to the ordinary person by putting its programmes on TV and radio and selling its course materials in bookshops. It has broken the monopoly power of conventional educational institutions.

The Open University did not at its inception twenty years ago set out to re-write the curriculum of higher education. As Birnbaum (1974) said

> *The Open University has begun with a fairly straightforward notion of subject matter which assumes that students have much to learn from an intact cultural tradition.*

Apart from putting knowledge into the public domain, it also was to make active use of the full range of the media for instruction in order to reach many more people without requiring vast capital sums to be spent on bricks and mortar. Behind this lay its social purpose, spelled out by the Planning Committee: (HMSO,1969)

> *For long regarded as a privilege of the few, the opportunity to engage in higher education is at last becoming widely accepted as a basic individual right* (Paragraph 6)

The objects of the Open University were laid down as:

> *To provide opportunities, at both undergraduate and post-graduate level, of higher education to all those who for any reason, have been or are being precluded from achieving their aims through an existing institution of higher education* (Paragraph 18)

The Open University was expected to press into the service of this cause all the existing teaching media and, over the years, to develop others. The OU and institutions like it worldwide have extended access to hundreds of thousands more learners through the intelligent use of technologies of delivery. There is no reason why the same methods should not assist the further education sector in extending its reach. The question is how further education can turn these trends to its own advantage, and use new and older technologies to reach more people in cost-effective and educationally desirable ways.

1.9 Access moves up the agenda

'Access' was not a matter of concern to most conventional institutions of higher education in the early 70s. Neither had there been any particular incentive to make more use of the media for degree level or further education/vocational work. The 1990s have seen an increase in participation rates and an increased interest in access particularly in the polytechnics, now 'new' universities. This has led to a significant growth in numbers of students and a concomitant pressure on staff, on teaching resources and space.

At the same time, the tidy vertically integrated single subject degree structures of the past are being changed into modular and more flexible patterns with arrangements for Credit Accumulation and Transfer between subject areas and institutions, a move promoted by the OU in the 70s. If degrees are broken into credit units or smaller modules, these do not need to be studied in linear consecutive form, or in one geographical place. One module may be studied or several, in a time and place of the learner's choice.

Developing Access (UDACE, 1988), a discussion paper on guidance and access, took a positive line and asked what a system *would need to be* in order to be perceived 'as an accessible system' by its users. In a useful analysis, they consider requirements for appropriate entry mechanisms, for the curriculum, for quality of support to individuals, for evaluation and monitoring and so on. At the end of the day what they are requiring is a thoroughly good and effective system. By definition such a system would have to be accessible! Indeed there are individual examples of such good institutions, but not yet enough of them.

Earlier on, the Leverhulme-funded study on Access to Higher Education (Fulton, 1981) made nine recommendations to improve access, several affecting further education, but movement on most of them has been minimal. They included among them six which are still relevant:

4. The sharp administrative and academic distinction between advanced and non-advanced courses should be abandoned.
5. Courses of higher and further education should be available to all those who can benefit from them and wish to do so. All admitting units should admit at least 25% of students using criteria other than A levels.
6. The universities and the CNAA should devise certificates of partial completion of degree courses, to be awarded after appropriate assessment.
7. The present grant system should be replaced with a system of 'educational entitlement' whereby every citizen is entitled to support for his or her education or training, regardless of its level.

8. All institutions, and especially those with highly competitive entry requirements, should undertake significant experiments with positive discrimination . . . When admitted, such students will need special support . . .
9. It should be the policy of government and of higher education institutions to encourage the participation of *adults* in courses of further and higher education at all levels, and to make appropriate provision for their special needs.

These recommendations have been quoted at length as a reminder since most of their recommendations and other important work in the area of access has not so far been implemented. It is not necessary to start from scratch and reinvent the policy wheel each decade. It is necessary for there to be enough political will and re-allocation of resources towards supporting increased access. While some institutions have made significant advances, many others have not, and the availability of provision is variable and therefore inequitable.

1.10 The provision of 'access' courses

Perhaps the most important development has been the increase in the provision of 'access' courses, usually provided through colleges of further education. The development of access courses has become an industry in itself: they have been validated since 1989 and around 40,000 further education students were enrolled on Access to HE courses in 1996–7. The on-line Access courses database contains 1,200 entries. Open College Networks (OCNs), who act as local accreditation/awarding bodies, work together within agreed quality standards through the National Open College Network (NOCN) and have become the largest awarding body for Schedule 2(d) courses.

Access courses are now included in the remit of the HE Quality Assurance Agency and the issue of Access Course Recognition has recently been reviewed by HEQC who have agreed to fund a modified arrangement focusing on the care and maintenance of the overall scheme through the licensing of the Authorised Validating Agencies (AVAs) which are responsible for the approval of individual Access courses and for the award of Access Certificates to students. It is now proposed that they will work to agreed national quality standards.

The coordinating work of the Access Course Recognition Group (ACRG) was until 1992 of particular importance in championing the importance of Access courses, and been continued under the HEQC. However, their positioning does raise problems of funding, standards and control. What level should they be at? Should there be national standards with an agreed currency? There is concern that they should not merely become an alternative barrier to access. One of their strengths has been the ability to develop in response to the needs of particular groups and localities, and to be matched to particular course and institutional needs. Some educators working locally tend to dismiss the need for a nationally agreed currency for access courses. While OCNS are collaborating in their accreditation within the National Open College Network, they are only beginning to operate through a shared national framework and certainly do not share a common curriculum. (Wilson,1997)

There is a real danger in the success of access courses, which is that their very existence becomes just another barrier to access. The over-organisation and accreditation of Access courses over the country as a whole brings the risk for adults that they simply become another rung on the ladder to be completed by everybody without conventional qualifications instead of A levels. This is a particular problem financially since while access courses are fundable through the FEFC, they are not eligible for mandatory grants, and discretionary grants in many areas have largely disappeared. Most access courses are modular and unitised and have been organised to enable part-time study under the 16-hour rule, which is now to be abolished. The original Gateway courses were, of course, also designed for part-time study, as is the Open University, and grants, therefore, although desirable for part-time study are not essential.

Understandably, the curriculum design of access courses has been varied to meet local needs and interests, particularly for specific disadvantaged groups. However, there are a lot of study elements in common across courses. A major limitation on any broadcaster who might be interested in collaborating with an Access course initiative (as a tele-course or distance learning course) is the lack of any nationally agreed framework of curriculum content for a programme series to work to. If national broadcasters were to provide resources for one or more access courses they would wish to work to a nationally agreed rubric and offer an open or distance learning study route with national accreditation. The National Extension College or the Open College of the Arts could be franchised to provide such distance learning access courses.

Indeed, the Open Polytechnic and the NEC tried unsuccessfully to get approval for a nationally available distance learning Access Course from the ACRG in 1990, but the approval structures all had to be locally based and to be locally delivered at that point. It is to be hoped that the new arrangements may allow for more flexible and responsive programmes and include distance learning in this.

In this context, it is worth noting that the first major set of what were effectively 'access' courses was provided by BBC Further Education together with the National Extension College as a preparation for the Open University in 1970/71. These preparatory or 'Gateway' courses as they became known (in Maths, Literature and History, and Social Science) were aimed at the open audience at home. Programmes were broadcast on radio and television, text books could be bought by post or in the bookshops, many colleges ran associated face-to-face tutorial courses and the National Extension College developed a correspondence course for each of the three series. It was impossible to measure exactly how many people followed those courses from the 'open audience', but some 7,000 returned the reply-paid questionnaire card inserted in the independent learning text books (McIntosh, 1971). Around one half were found to be 'highly likely' to enrol for the Open University. The Associated Examining Board provided an optional assessment for those who wanted certification. Those who had completed preparatory courses, and who then went on to join the OU, passed their Open University foundation courses at significantly higher rates than other students.

The 'Gateway' courses were only broadcast for two years though the materials continued in demand for a long time; and the courses undoubtedly would have continued to interest potential students for many years. The BBC would not at that point commit schedule-time out of its regular FE slots for more than two years. However, with digital television more channel space is soon to arrive and the possibility of such nationally available access courses is an interesting option to re-visit.

Although broadcasters are not likely to wish to develop programme series which are specifically designed only for access to particular institutions or for particular localities – these could be more suitable for cable or narrowcasting – there are some programme areas which are likely to interest a broader adult audience as well as being appropriate as a foundation for more systematic study.

1.11 Experience of broadcast-led telecourses

The strength of broadcasting is that it can reach out to people in their own homes, who may not yet know what they want, and engage their interest. It is a very powerful engine for major collaborative projects with education institutions: the BBC's first Schools Computer Project in the 70s, the initial Adult Literacy campaign, and this year's IT Awareness campaign are all examples, as Alan Tuckett records in his companion paper. (Tuckett, 1997)

There is now quite widespread experience in running telecourses. In America, the concept of telecourses is well-known and accepted, as is their use of credit structures of qualifications post-school. Apart from Annenberg-supported telecourses, many local PBS stations and colleges and universities collaborate to enable registered students to study telecourses for credit, usually as part of associate or bachelor degrees. The UK has no real equivalent, though it is interesting that two of Channel 4's series *The World- A Television History* and *Planet Earth* were adopted by South Carolina's PBS station who developed specially designed US telecourses to accompany them and offered them through the PBS Adult Learning Service. Channel 4's two astronomy series fronted by Heather Couper have similarly been built on for systematic learning through broadcasting by Teleac in Holland. Nearer home, and as a run-up to the setting up of the Open College, Channel 4 worked with Yorkshire Television and BTEC to develop telecourses in the area of marketing and economics as part of BTEC's modular Certificate of Business Administration. Television-led projects can also make a serious contribution at the Basic Skills level as the BBC, Channel 4 and Yorkshire Television have all shown.

It is more difficult to know at what level and for what qualifications one could pitch telecourses led by major arts or history series, but this should be a possibility. UK examples which could have led to accreditation in the US were Channel 4/LWTs *Ten Great Writers* and TVS/Annenberg's *Art of the Western World*, which has indeed subsequently been integrated into an open learning course by the Open College of the Arts.

1.12 The need for appropriate adult non-vocational qualifications

Many people have left and still leave school at 16 and wish to return to education later on in life. They need a pattern of relevant qualifications which have currency both for educators and for employers. The widespread provision of access courses and the development of OCN networks is helpful, but these do not provide a linking or broad enough framework. What is needed is a proper and broad array of qualifications suitable for adults. 'A' levels and other school-level qualifications are not structured nor is the curriculum necessarily appropriate for adults and, for many people, does not offer an appropriate progression route.

It has been a matter of major concern to those engaged in the education of adults that the merger of SCAA and NCVQ has been carried through without any consideration of its implications for the wider educational and accreditation needs of adults. Of course, as Peter Newsam would remind us, the education industry is dominated by those with a background in school-level work. They think about adults only as an afterthought. Adults deserve a forethought as new qualifications structures are developed if lifelong learning is to become a reality. Broadcasters might then have a framework to gear their more systematic offerings to and broadcast resources could be put to increased use. These could genuinely provide a new point of access for many adults and probably help many colleges and sixth forms with resource materials as well.

2 Open and distance learning

2.1 The growth of open and distance learning

Using new technologies of any sort usually involves utilising some form of open and distance learning methods. The place of study is, for many learners, a matter of extreme importance. Most adult learners study part-time. Open and distance learning has proved particularly helpful in reaching part-time learners who are in work, in reaching geographically isolated students, in reaching people, mainly women, who are tied to the home, people working unsocial hours or in unsocial jobs, people in prison etc.

But it is not just a rescue mission: it is important simply because people can choose how they wish to study and fit it in with their other obligations. This flexibility is likely to be of increased importance as more adult learners need to come in and out of education and training opportunities throughout their adult lives.

The OU, for example, continues to attract many people who might otherwise go to conventional universities or colleges mainly because it offers to the learner the choice about how, when and where to learn, even if it is becoming increasingly expensive and a very demanding way to study.

2.2 Definitions and descriptions used in open and distance learning

It is sensible to clarify the terminology first. The use and acceptability of different terms has more to do with the sector of education and training using the term, and its habits and prejudices, and less to do with intrinsic differences which matter. A useful general description of open learning is :

> *Open learning describes ways of helping individuals to take advantage of their own learning. Learners may, for example, choose:*
>
> *– what they learn (content)*
> *– how they learn (methods, media, routes)*
> *– where they learn (place)*
> *– when they learn (time)*
> *– how quickly they learn (pace)*
> *– who to turn to for help*
> *– whether, when, where to have their learning assessed*
> (Lewis & McDonald, 1989)

The term 'open learning' is more commonly used in further and higher education and in industry, but it is not necessarily learning 'at a distance'. What differentiates 'distance learning' and its main proponent the Open University as the foremost example of this, is that the learner is 'at a distance' from the designer/provider of the intellectual materials.

The EC memorandum on the subject simply uses the portmanteau term Open Distance Learning (Com 91–388). The EC memorandum is helpful in its extended definition.

> *Distance learning is defined as any form of study not under the continuous or immediate supervision of tutors, but which nevertheless benefits from the planning, guidance and tuition of a tutorial organisation. Distance learning has a large component of independent or autonomous learning and is therefore heavily dependent on the didactic design of materials which must substitute for the interactivity available between student and teacher in ordinary face-to-face instruction. The*

> *autonomous component is invariably supported by tutoring and counselling systems which ideally are provided at regional/local study centres and to an increasing extent by modern communications media. Because open distance learning is meant to be adaptable to the pace of the student, the material is generally structured in units or modules geared to specific learning outcomes.* Com (91):388 Para 15

The UK has become the world leader in the development of distance learning, and has similarly taken the lead in Europe in relation to 'open learning', now an EC priority. Distance and open learning techniques, as noted earlier, have proved particularly valuable for busy, mature and motivated adults. It is no accident that the Manpower Services Commission and the subsequent training arms of the Employment Department made it deliberate policy to promote open learning as a valuable and economic means of training adults, funding both the Open Tech initiative and the Open College to develop new resources in order to reach new learners. The MSC/TA/ED support for open learning, coming as it did from outside the educational system, has been successful in legitimating it and embedding it in a number of, mainly large, companies as well as in many education and training institutions. The view is increasingly held that it will not be possible for the UK to reach the National Training and Education Targets without the use of open and distance learning methods.

Developments have included a regularly updated Open Learning directory, regular conferences attracting participants from both industry and education and training, Open Learning Resource Centres in many colleges and public libraries, and the entry into the field of a number of commercial publishers. Indeed, Pearson Professional has recently acquired the commercial interest in the Open College and its intellectual property. There is now an active Open Learning Federation with 450 members, 40% of whom are individual members and 60% organisations, mainly FE colleges and companies.

The British Association for Open Learning has also developed rapidly with members mainly representing developers and distributors of learning materials but including FE colleges, TECs and corporate users. It is working on encouraging the use of quality assurance standards for the development and use of open learning. The picture among Training and Enterprise Councils (TECs) is more varied: with their local remits, they have less incentive to collaborate in the provision and use of resources. However, several TECs have developed their own resource centres mainly aimed at small and medium-sized enterprises and other local employers.

Open, distance and flexible learning have more recently been given a boost by the new FEFC funding arrangements which provide the same unit of resource for such learning as for conventionally taught programmes. Many colleges now have open learning centres, providing flexible access to learning support. Increasingly employers are also providing such centres, sometimes staffed by their local FE college. The Employment Department, now merged into the DfEE, has been encouraging the development of open learning centres in public libraries.

A number of colleges have successfully undertaken innovative developments in the delivery of computer-based learning, including Halton College which has developed its own multi-media production facilities. Other examples are Wirral Metropolitan College which has combined network-delivered resources with practical workshop activity, Skelmersdale College which is supporting large numbers of adult students studying at a distance for an IT vocational qualification and Luton Sixth Form College which has extablished computer-based learning resource centres and electronic self-testing for GNVQ students.

At school level, 'flexible learning' and 'supported self-study' are terms more commonly used and found acceptable by school-teachers. In particular, the Employment Department funded TVEI initiative in schools used the term 'flexible learning'. TVEI money was often used to fund the development of IT in schools which was often associated with the use of flexible learning.

2.3 Development and diversification

It is helpful to understand the options that organisations and businesses have for diversification and the possible reasons for suggesting setting up a new organisation. A useful framework from industry against which to test the objects of innovation and growth has also proved helpful in analysing educational innovations. Ansoff's classic matrix argues that a company has effectively only four options in pursuit of growth: it can sell more of its products to existing markets (market penetration), more of its existing products to new markets (market development), develop new products for existing markets (product development) or develop new products for new markets (diversification). (Ansoff,1965) Using Ansoff's matrix as a model for the educational system at the time of the setting up of the OU was illuminating.

Product / Mission	Present	New
Present	Existing institutions Existing students	New institutions Existing students, eg, polytechnics
New	Existing institutions New students eg, Sussex University	New institutions New students, eg, the Open University

Figure 2: Higher education in the UK in the late 60s

Until the late sixties, in principle, the demand for higher education from conventionally qualified 18-21-year-old full-time students was met through universities: while several new universities had been set up following the Robbins Report, their mission was definitely to provide for 'more of the same' students. The polytechnics were also being established, albeit as a new type of institution, predominantly to meet the needs of the same market, the 18-21 year olds fresh from school seeking degrees. Neither were many of the existing universities trying to move into new markets: a notable exception was Sussex who had made a commitment to take in a number of unqualified and mature students.

The strategy for diversification selected for the Open University in 1969 by the Government of the day was two-fold: it was to be a new institution (product) and to reach new learners (markets), in the form of mature and unqualified learners, particularly women and the working class. It is not always sensible or necessary to set up a new institution to reach new learners. It will depend on such things as the existing educational investment and infrastructure, possible competition and the size of the potential market. Where existing investment in education and training in terms of money, people and plant is already high, it may be less important to set up a new institution than for existing institutions to be more flexible and reach out to new students.

An individual institution faces the same choices in terms of diversification as the system does as a whole. It can continue to teach its existing students but use new ways, it can teach new students in existing ways, or it can aim to teach new students in new ways. The OU at its inception was not only interested in reaching new students, ie, the mature, including those unqualified, but it was also set up specifically to teach in 'new' ways and to make active use of the full range of existing media for its instruction. The media were to be used to reach people who could not be reached in conventional ways, and to enable larger numbers of people to be taught at lower cost. It also relied heavily, and still does, on older, lower-tech ways such as print which are still extremely cheap and cost-effective, and continues to use a mix of old and new technologies, from TV and radio to the Internet.

Students / Ways	Present	New
Present	Existing students Existing ways	New students Existing ways
New	Existing students New ways	New students New ways

Figure 3: types of students and ways of study

The saving of resources with using the media comes, as noted earlier, from delivering one centrally produced message. The message can be personalised in a number of ways, though the more this is done, the more it may cost. Options for personalising messages include face-to-face contact, phone, telex, audio-cassette, post, fax and electronic mail. New technologies have assisted in the development of new and more flexible forms of ODL, involving greater use of these more 'personal media'. They enable individual contact between tutors and students and also between students and other students. At the same time these trends move more of the cost of access away from the providing institution and on to the learner.

Another key variable is the course of study. Switching from 'ways of learning' to 'courses of study' focuses on whether the goal is to make existing courses available to 'new' students, or to produce new courses for existing students or both. To complete the analysis satisfactorily, it is necessary to develop a multi-dimensional matrix across a number of characteristics of learning systems, noting the 'newness' or not of the characteristics, and the objectives to be achieved.

Learning characteristics	***Existing/new***	***Objective***
Types of students		
Course materials		
Delivery systems		
Location of learning		
Learning support		
Qualifications		
Accreditation		

Figure 4: Characteristics of learning systems

'New' students can, of course, be of different sorts: women returners, employees at work, minority ethnic groups, those with basic skills needs and so on. Some delivery systems are more suitable for some groups than others. This diversification matrix provides a helpful framework against which to consider the rationale for and criteria of success of previous innovative developments in the UK. Apart from the use of new media within existing institutions, there are and have already been a number of 'new' institutions set up aiming to use new technologies or make better use of existing technologies: the main ones reviewed here are the OU, the Open College, the Open Tech, the Open Learning Foundation and the National Extension College.

2.4 Learning from other initiatives: competition or collaboration

There are lessons to be learnt from the experience of these previous initiatives which are of help in the planning of any major new national initiative or network.

A number of questions may be asked about previous and current projects:

- who is/was it aimed at?
- what were its original objectives, and how did it expect to fulfil them?
- what qualifications did/does it offer, if any?
- what types of materials and delivery mechanisms did it use?
- how is/was it funded?
- how is its quality rated?
- how does it relate to existing institutions?
- what has hindered its progress?
- what useful lessons can be learnt from its experience?

Using technology, whether for networking or for the delivery of distance learning, is expensive up-front and requires investment in both software and hardware. This usually requires the justification of reaching large numbers, as with the OU, or collaboration between institutions as with the Open Learning Foundation (OLF). The financial burden can also be spread, and the risk shared, through commercial production or through partnerships, both of which enable larger groups to be served cost-effectively, since resources can be bought in small amounts by individual institutions. However, current structures are designed to encourage competition rather than collaboration.

The other relevant trends are towards down-sizing and outsourcing, combined with the principle of individuals purchasing services from providers. The tension between these options is not assisted by the well-known 'not invented here' syndrome which prevents many academics using other institutions' course materials, no matter how good or cheap.

2.5 The Open Learning Foundation – a model of collaboration

The Open Learning Foundation (originally the Open Polytechnic) has set itself to work collaboratively. Although some individual polytechnics had involved themselves in open learning over the decade, sometimes as a result of Open Tech projects, many had not, nor was there any network of collaboration between those that did – if anything, there was competition. At the same time an increasing number of polytechnic staff were being commissioned by the OU to write course materials, particularly as the OU started to expand into areas such as Management and Business Studies, areas which had previously been polytechnic territory. Many polytechnics already housed OU Study Centres and also provided many of its part-time tutors. While to some this looked like symbiosis, to others it looked like exploitation, and within this lay some of the seeds of the idea of the Open Polytechnic, set up in 1990. What is surprising is that the ex-Polytechnic sector did not make such a move many years earlier – previous attempts had mainly foundered on competitiveness between institutions. After all, many polytechnics have been in the forefront of innovation in curriculum and access terms and also have available a wide array of audio-visual resources.

The Open Polytechnic was not set up to be a new institution registering its own students but a consortium of 21 members of the sector who had agreed to work together to 'harness existing resources to reach very large numbers of students'. Initial capital was provided by subscriptions from each member entitling them to have access to its services and materials at members' rates. The blueprint emphasised high-quality, mixed-mode opportunities, the opening up of access, opportunities for staff development as well as, more pragmatically, opportunities for cost-cutting and income generation. The strategy was to provide course resources, mainly print, for staff to choose to use in their teaching, rather than for students to choose to use for independent learning. (Sargant,1991)

It now has nearly 30 members giving it the potential of reaching some 400,000 students though its materials are not yet very widely used. Its main content areas include business studies, management, hospitality studies, social work, engineering and health and nursing. But it is a teaching-staff led rather than a learner-led model, and is effectively more like a publishing house. It offers its members access to a wide range of learning materials at preferential rates. It has been sufficiently successful in selling materials and raising additional co-production resources to halve the members' regular subscriptions from the initial £25,000, but the adequacy of the costing mechanisms and pay-back systems is still not clear.

What it does offer to its members is participation in the development of materials, including nominating authors and editors from among the member institutions' own staff. Though this adds to development time, the gain in terms of acceptability and transferability to other members is very significant and overcomes some of the difficulties the Open Tech Initiative experienced. It is increasingly assisting its members in the development of their own learning materials, often on a paid consultancy basis.

The OLF is basically a publisher/provider of degree-level independent learning resources, and many of these are likely to be suitable for further education and for work-related learning outside education institutions. Some areas have been developed in collaboration with professional bodies, eg, Health Services Management and Social Work and there is an increasing overlap in the vocational and professional areas between higher and further education.

It has not made the use of new (or older) technologies a priority, and most of its courses are print-based, though they are mainly distributed on disc under licence rather than in print. An interesting development is the piloting of the distribution of materials on electronic networks and on-demand electronic publishing. It does not register or teach students: this is done through member organisations. However, its aim continues to be to increase access and serve a more diverse learner clientele. Its course materials fit within the HE CATS framework. It is now arranging for independent credit rating of its learning materials where appropriate, so that they can be used by individual learners, eg, for continuing professional development (CPD).

In conclusion, the proposal which found favour among peers in polytechnics was not to set up a new competitive institution, but to set up a consortium of polytechnics to collaborate to produce new learning resources to assist existing polytechnics and colleges to teach existing students in new, more flexible and economic ways (see Figure 5). The emphasis was less on access than on the efficient and cost-effective management of teaching. However, using new resources to deliver learning is likely to, as a next stage, enable new courses to be developed and should also open up access to new learners.

This could well be a sensible route for the FE system to take. There are a number of areas where high quality learning resources could be developed for use nationally: basic skills materials, ESOL, business studies and accountancy, for example, and there are significant materials already available at this level from other open learning providers such as the Open College or the National Extension College which could be bought in bulk for a network at this level.

Existing students Existing resources	Existing students New resources
New students Existing resources	New students New resources

Figure 5: New resources for increased access

2.6 The Open Tech Programme: a funding mechanism

Two other '80s initiatives are particularly relevant for further education, as they were both expected to use media and their goals are still current priorities. The first, The Open Tech Programme, was primarily a funding initiative rather than an institution, and the second, the Open College, was again a free-standing institution aimed at using broadcasting and at being a lower-level vocational analogue to the OU.

Jim Prior, as Secretary of State for Employment, had been interested in setting up an analogue to the OU 'to meet adult training and retraining needs at technician and related levels', and after the publication of a consultation document in May 1981, a Task Group was set up to plan what was to be called *The Open Tech Programme*. (MSC,1981) It was not to be a new institution, but a 'planned and co-ordinated range of commissioned projects'. The Programme was described as having two key tasks:

- to open or widen access to existing training provision
- to make new education and training provision which from the beginning can best be met through open learning.

It was to focus primarily on technical and supervisory skills as this was regarded as a key area for economic growth. It was not set up as a new institution but as a **funding mechanism** which aimed to encourage the development of open learning materials to be widely available across the country, building on local expertise in the training and technical field. The programme was to be funded for a limited period of four years, launched in August 1982 and to end in March 1987. The programme had a total government budget of £45 million, which was used to support a wide variety of open/distance learning projects primarily concerned with adult technical training, 80% of the funds being allocated to technical projects, and 20% to supervisory and management training. The programme was designed to build upon existing resources and not establish new competitive institutions. The needs of the learner were to be regarded as central: the system must adapt to the learner rather than vice versa.

Money was provided centrally by the MSC to fund these locally developed open learning initiatives, but they were not controlled within an overall intellectual, curriculum content and quality framework. Yeats (1986) in an assessment of the scheme describes it in these words:

OTP is a decentralised project system. It involves the development of a wide range of materials, delivery, support and practical 'hands on' projects by a large number of contracted bodies.

It is difficult for any such project to ascertain what are the most relevant current and future training needs. Manpower forecasts available were considered too broad and general. The shortage of information, Yeats notes, led economists in the Training Services division of MSC to advise (in a somewhat defeatist way!):

> *The best way into the problem of determining what needs for supervisory or technician training exist and what their nature may be is probably to follow up and examine more closely the needs signalled in submissions for OTP.* (MSC, 1982:16)

Its programme objectives as described are virtually identical to those of the proposed University for Industry and several also relate closely to the role of further education if the national NTETs targets are to be achieved. Yeats records five objectives:

a. Meeting the needs of changing labour market demands
b. Meeting the employment needs and aspirations of individuals
c. Responding to technological change and innovation
d. Applying and demonstrating the role of open learning in vocational education and training
e. Increasing the flexibility of the education and training system

The lack of a defining national framework appears to have been deliberate. Yeats notes that 'It is difficult to say exactly what has been achieved so far . . . . no agreement exists as to what constitutes a learning unit, or even a learning hour of student time'. Most surprising, and markedly different to the present day, was the virtual lack of any attention paid to the issue of qualifications. Not until April 1985 was a Working Group established to enquire into the current situation regarding vocational qualifications. When it reported in April 1986, its main recommendation was that the Government should establish a National Council for Vocational Qualifications (NCVQ).

The absence of a national framework of standards and accreditation meant that course materials were not readily accepted by others as transferable and usable in other places and situations. Indeed, it appeared to be policy for them NOT to be national in their goals – a policy which caused both their chiefs in turn to refuse the free offer of supporting national broadcasting made to them by the newly set up Channel 4.

As the Open Tech was set up as a 'temporary system', projects were given three-year funding and were then expected to become self-sustaining based 'on the assumption that adults retraining through the Open Tech Programme would have to pay for their own self improvement.' (Ainley and Corney, 1990)

As with further education, the Open Tech was also given a social objective, that all OTP projects should be fully available to members of 'special groups' – the unemployed, the disabled, ethnic minorities and women. In the event, only seven projects aimed, for example, at the unemployed. When projects have to survive in a competitive market, Yeats notes, it will be difficult for such 'special groups' to take advantage of the new training opportunities offered without additional financial help.

Projects funded were of three main types: materials development projects, delivery projects, and support projects, eg, in staff training, marketing, information supply (MARIS) and evaluation and these were considered an important factor in its early success. For example, many people involved in materials production were inexperienced in distance learning techniques and in the operational aspects of open learning projects and the Open Tech Training and Support Unit provided such support. A similar need for such staff training has been experienced by the Open Learning Foundation.

The vast majority, 120 out of the 140 projects funded, were for materials development with much less emphasis on their marketing, delivery and learning support. There was evidence that many projects had little or no idea as to how they would deliver their materials after they had produced them.

Yeats identifies a number of relevant effects. The project suffered from its short programme life. It was more difficult to get projects going in industry and education got in earlier, with 61% of the money going to education and 23% to industry. The degree of collaboration between the two was disappointing. The hoped-for effects of encouraging the industrial sector to take more responsibility for the education and training of workers was only partly achieved.

More specific problems on the industry side noted were possible difficulties with industrial relations in setting up an open learning unit, the issue of the cost effectiveness of open learning, the difficulty of companies collaborating in areas where they would normally compete, and an 'access' issue of how open a company can be to non-employees.

Though technology was regarded as central to the project, this turned out to be observed more in theory than in practice, as with the refusal to use national broadcasting. In the event print continued to be the most important medium, as it has been with the OLF. 'The technology is being emphasised and used more because it is available, rather than for any proven pedagogical superiority.' (Yeats) His report also raises the important issue of adequate access to centres for practical skills training and assessment provision.

At the same time, however, the MSC did set up an in-house Learning Technology Unit in parallel to the Open Tech Programme which supported a number of developments of computer-based learning, including Project Author. The unit's work provided training for a new generation of computer-based training designers and authors who contributed to the establishment and growth of many CBT companies in the 1980s. The unit saw itself as encouraging the development of leading edge applications, some of which sadly did not get beyond the blueprint stage, but several did produce significant outcomes which influenced the design and approach taken by later producers of CBT.

A small number of specific Open Tech projects have survived and been the origin of, for example, the Cleveland Open Learning Unit and the Birmingham Open Learning Development Unit, but a lot sank without trace, and many institutions, it is claimed, simply took the money and ran. However, the current network of learning producers and distributors contains many individuals who developed their skills working on Open Tech projects. Some Open Tech projects re-emerged alongside other new such as the Open Learning Foundation.

The Open Tech Programme has been considered in some detail since its objectives are still relevant to further education and it offers an alternative strategy for change. It has not generated much in the way of lasting materials, but it has resulted in a larger number of people with skills and experience of developing and delivering open learning materials, many of them working in the FE sector. It did not, however, focus adequately on delivery to learners.

It is possible that such an initiative, given the more general acceptance of open learning and the slow, but increasing, coherence of national vocational qualifications might now have a better chance of succeeding. Arguably, it was in advance of its time. Its impetus, presumably, was to allow local ownership of more modestly produced materials than the OU's, and to avoid the 'not invented here' syndrome. However, the Catch 22 is that economy in developing such resources only arises from their use with large numbers of learners and requires transferability of credit/accreditation. It did, therefore, have built-in seeds of failure and few materials were used elsewhere.

To set up a model of this sort for further education would require much tighter control of commissioning, of curriculum, assessment, quality and accreditation to ensure transferability of materials and of qualifications and credit. It could also be useful for modest cost initiatives in, say, one TEC or in a group of linked TEC areas, particularly where a cable network or a regional ITV company might be interested in collaborating.

2.7 The Open College: a new institution

In 1986 the Training Agency, supported by the Department of Employment, made another serious attempt to use the media to enhance education and training opportunities specifically at further education level. Just as the OU was set up to make alternative provision for higher (degree-level) education, the Open College was originally planned to make the 'curriculum of a good FE college' available to adults who needed to bridge the 16-19 level gap, and thereby to make a contribution to updating and re-skilling the adult population, including, importantly, the unemployed.

Subsidiary goals were to simplify the maze of overlapping vocational qualifications, modernise the apprenticeship system and encourage credit accumulation and transfer systems. Funding was to come from the Employment Department.

Airtime for the main broadcast component had again been offered by Channel 4 – at lunch-time across the weekdays – a time slot which was good for the unemployed and offered an interesting opportunity to work with employers and unions in new workplace-based study opportunities. Colleges would also be able to video-record programmes to add to their bank of learning resources at minimum cost, as well as running some day-time courses.

Government priorities at the time were to over-ride those plans and it determined that the Open College should not try to reach the unemployed, but only deliver vocational education and training to those already in work. This removed at a stroke the rationale for Channel 4's offer of the lunch-time slot, and also removed the numerical justification of large numbers of the unemployed, thus making it impossible to meet the College's original targets, and limiting its potential usefulness. In a similar decision, the government ruled out the provision of GCSE courses, which the OC's own market research had shown was the qualification most recognised and desired by adults and and which OC management considered would be a 'comfortable and fruitful' area for investment as it would also attract adults as parents.

Research showed that the Channel 4 broadcasting was initially very effective in raising the level of awareness of the Open College and in stimulating people to seek out Open College learning centres which were located mainly in further education colleges. The timetable had allowed 15 months from start of planning to going on air, but some months were lost getting staff in post. The initial array of courses available was, inevitably, thin and many students who had been stimulated by television to enquire at colleges were seeking courses the OC did not provide. There was also apocryphal evidence of some colleges who simply enrolled the enquiring students on their own courses rather than directing them on to OC courses. Numbers were slow to build up but, two years in, David Grugeon reports that over 30,000 had been recruited through OC Gateway Centres and a further 10,000 through the Open College's (subsequently set up) direct recruitment agency.

The exclusion of the unemployed had not only reduced the numbers available to be reached, but also precluded the use of existing general educational programming material for adults, which Channel 4 had offered the OC as a form of additional subsidy. A further negative factor affecting broadcasting was the tightness of the rules concerning sponsorship of broadcast programmes, and the unexpected unavailability of sponsorship money.

Four years in, after a Government-required review of the College, funding for the broadcast element was withdrawn and the main broadcasting element on Channel 4 ceased, though some other audio-visual support for courses continues. The Government continued to 'capitalise' the college for a further three years during which time it invested heavily in the production of new course materials for onward sales essentially as a publishing house. In 1992, the College made a further, though unsuccessful, bid to the Employment Department for broadcasting time, but to use it for marketing open learning activities and opportunities.

Concentrating on the commissioning and development of high quality open learning materials, the OC succeeded in re-establishing itself as a provider of learning resources and support rather than as a College in the conventional sense and is now a substantial business. It has focused successfully on the corporate market and is a major provider to several blue-chip companies. It delivers a whole range of programmes to public and private organisations in the technical, management and health-care field, and by 1996 was providing open/flexible learning to about 2,000 workplace learners in 152 programmes through 61 different employers. It has 63 part-time, Open College-trained tutors. Almost all of its course materials lead to national accreditation, 20% of which is straight NVQ-based, with the balance leading to traditional qualifications.

It is also now a sizeable publishing house of open and flexible learning material (OFL), probably the second largest after the OU, and probably the largest supplier of OFL to the FE and HE sectors for their own use. 66,757 modules of OC OFL materials had been sold since the start of 1995, and this will increase to 80,000 modules by the end of 1996. Materials have been bought by 560-odd customers, of whom 150 are regular buyers and are providers of OFL training themselves, either HE, FE or 'other providers'. Materials can be bought, used under licence or franchise. TECs and companies make them available through Open Learning Centres, for example. In this way, it is likely that about another 16,000 learners are being tutored and supported by other institutions using Open College materials.

Publishing revenue is now about a quarter of total revenue of £4-5 million. Open learning materials are available for Supervision, Management, Portfolio Development, Training for Trainers and Work Skills and Health and Care and others. Its new nursing materials are to be endorsed by the Royal College of Nursing (RCN). The latest news of its future is that the College's commercial operation has been bought up by Pearson Professional and been separated from its public sector originated charitable foundation – a version of delayed privatisation!

As with FE colleges, the Open College was not set up with its own accreditation powers, and this was seen earlier on to be a limitation not experienced by the polytechnics or the OU. It now chooses to provide course materials for a wide variety of qualifications and their validating bodies, eg, EdExcel, City & Guilds and RSA. Its experience has been that different companies/industries are specific in their requirements for, and loyalty to, particular qualifications and the college could better serve people by offering a range of qualifications. As a national body, it could have chosen to be an NVQ Awarding Body, but decided against it for the reason given above. However, it is also now linking to the Oxford University Delegacy for local exams for some accreditation purposes.

Since government subsidy was withdrawn, the College has been able to operate completely independently, building up to a turnover of approaching £4 million a year, some 56,000 learners will have used College developed OFL materials, and over 350,000 modules of materials have been sold. It has run until now as a company limited by guarantee, though it did not make its Annual Report available. Its former Chief Executive commented that it was operating in a very competitive market.

The reputation of the Open College still suffers from its early difficulties; it has been much more successful than most people realise and provides some key lessons for a future structure, as well as being a source of existing materials. Though its work with larger corporate users is encouraging, it has had to target the most efficient means of being self-funding. Whilst it does not have large numbers of SME users or independent learners directly registered with it, these categories have benefited from using its materials through other sources such as FE colleges and TECs, who are both currently considering new ways of reaching SMEs.

A major problem is the confusing plethora of qualifications at FE level which are not as 'desirable' or easily saleable as a degree. Despite good, systematic use of market research to aid its planning, the OC's experience has been that there are few content areas which generate a demand for more than 3,500 copies of a course. These numbers do not bode well for colleges, even in collaboration.

The assessment of competence-based qualifications presents particular difficulties with open and distance learning. With the development of NVQs, the Open College has spent *'considerable resource on the implementation of competence-based programmes and has developed a specific niche in helping organisations to implement standards for staff to obtain associated units and components of NVQs.'* John Trasler, its MD, suggests that its strength lies in helping organisations to implement some of the national training targets by devising non-bureaucratic systems which meet the needs both of business and individuals.

There is much to be learnt from the OC's experience, particularly in its use of open and distance learning and its commissioning and quality control of courses. There should be ways in which further education could make better use of its existing courses and perhaps develop appropriate partnerships to commission and deliver new courses, though the OC's new commercial status may make this more difficult.

Colleges are particularly well-placed to provide learning support for open and distance learners. Initially with the Open College there were real problems of competition with colleges enrolling potential OC students in their own programmes. However, as the NEC has shown with its various schemes with colleges, there are possible methods of collaboration which benefit both sides.

John Trasler, who remains its Managing Director, offers the following OC up-date:

> *The recognition of its success in the corporate training market was shown by its acquisition by Pearson plc in February 1997. The Open College Ltd still focuses on business-driven training and development and now has access to a wider range of intellectual copyright and investment for new material. It has continued to develop open learning, investing in an Internet capability and delivery of learning by such media.*
>
> *The Open College's new commercial status is not in reality any different from the position it has occupied for the last five years and there are many ways in which its material could be used in the further education and SME sectors. In conjunction with Pearson Professional companies, it is also keen to support and promote the University for Industry.*

2.8 The National Extension College: a partnership model

NEC is an independent, non-profit-making distance learning college, originally set up by Michael Young (Lord Young of Dartington) in 1963. Michael Young appears to be the first person to have used the term 'open university' in an article in *Where* magazine in 1962 in which he proposed an 'open university' to prepare people for external degrees of London University, many of whom were receiving poor teaching from private correspondence colleges.

In referring to such overseas experience as the Soviet Correspondence Colleges and educational television in the US, he proposed the need for a National Extension College to act as the nucleus of an 'open university' with three main functions: to organise new and better correspondence courses for the external degree, to promote lectures and residential schools (working through the extra-mural departments of London and other universities), and to teach by means of television.

NEC is constituted as a Company Limited by Guarantee and, while surviving a number of financial vicissitudes, has managed without any regular grants or subsidy all its life. It was determined to be more ethical than the private correspondence colleges of those years who were renowned for making their money, as Colmans, from the mustard left on the side of the plate, ie, the learners who paid their fees in advance and then dropped out without completing their course.

Its materials are extremely high quality and are widely used in school and colleges. They are available as courses, as flexible resources or through the purchase of a photocopying licence. It offers a personal tutorial service for its distance learners as part of its package, including assessment arrangements with appropriate examination authorities.

NEC currently provides over 150 courses with personal support through distance learning. Over 15,000 adults enrol each year, either to gain new skills or qualifications or to boost confidence or career opportunities. NEC estimates that nearly 400,000 students have enrolled with it since it was set up in 1963.

In 1995, 80% of students were enrolled on basic or academic and general education courses, 15% on vocational courses, mainly NVQ or equivalent, and 5% on degree, Engineering Council or Institute of Linguist qualifications through directed private study. In addition, it provides a personal tutorial service for London External Degrees.

The majority of its work is for adults, at FE or schools examination level. It has a broad portfolio of courses for adults who want to catch up on previously missed chances from basic skills to GCSE and A levels. It also has an increasing vocational and professional portfolio. As the Open College, much of its business is as a publishing house, selling particularly to FE colleges. It sold over 30,000 packs in 1995, 50% of which were academic and general education, 15% were basic education, 12% were languages, 6% training materials for staff development and 17% NVQ-related materials in Accounting, Administration and Care. In addition, it provides a personal tutorial service for London University External degrees.

It works with other education providers and advisory services to assist progression and accreditation. It also works with major employers such as Ford, Lucas, BT, Mercury, Cable & Wireless, the Post Office and the Stock Exchange. NEC notes that employers are becoming more active in sponsoring learners, either through group schemes or in response to an individual's request to take a course. It has recently set up an exciting new in-company training scheme for Coca-Cola Schweppes to enable school-leavers to obtain a degree in Management while pursuing a full-time career in merchandising. The degree element of the scheme has been set up as an open learning scheme through NEC and Bradford University.

Its array of course materials are clearly of interest to further education, together with its capacity for developing independent learning materials. In 1994, it set up a pilot project with a group of 12 FE colleges to explore the possibilities of a partnership arrangement which would enable the FE colleges to offer NEC's distance learning courses to their students. Called the CoNECt (Colleges and NEC together) scheme, it provides a cost-effective way for colleges to extend their curriculum offer to students and enable them to enrol those individuals who are not able to study on-site. It means they can offer more flexible modes of delivery and offer options for year-round enrolment and self-pacing study. The scheme means that each college does not have to keep its course materials updated for its students, or establish the complex administrative and computer systems necessary to enrol and monitor distance learning students or recruit and train distance learning tutors in all subject areas. Colleges provide pre-entry advice and guidance, access to non-tutorial learner support and study facilities, and assessment and examination processes.

It is starting to produce its materials in multi-media formats as well as print. It provides a competent and conscientious personal tutorial service and research shows a high degree of loyalty and repeat purchase among its learners. It could provide an independent learning tutorial service for a network. It has a strong track record of innovation, providing both courses for independent learners with tutorial support and also a wide variety of open learning resources for institutions. Most important is that, as the Open College does, it works to much lower cost levels and to much faster time-scales than the OU.

2.9 General lessons of previous relevant initiatives

This brief survey of previous initiatives highlights their similarities and differences and some of their strengths and weaknesses. What is clear is that working at further education and often vocational levels provides a greater challenge for open and distance learning since there is a greater variety of qualifications and a greater need for work-place relevance and delivery to new clienteles and to new milieux.

There are some recurring issues which any new project will also face:

- it is difficult to ascertain/research the most relevant current and future training needs, to discover where the numbers justify using technologies
- using technology requires a longer lead-time and guaranteed funding. 'Short-term' money or money with strings has caused problems with previous projects
- there is a need for a unified national framework of qualifications to ensure quality and transferability of credit
- along with this is the need for proper accreditation systems
- the need for staff development: for materials production and for running open learning operations
- the need for ownership of materials and the 'not invented here' syndrome militate against collaboration
- the appropriateness and availability of new technologies. Despite the apparent promises of new technology, print/post continues to be the most important technology of delivery
- increasing competition between providers.

For learners:

- the provision of independent guidance
- the need for learning support and individualised tutorial support
- the sense of being in a community
- guaranteed quality and coherence of the system.

For companies:

- the cost-effectiveness of open learning
- difficulties of companies collaborating instead of competing
- companies offering access to people outside their company
- companies providing time-off from work for study.

There are some benefits that have been derived from these initiatives;

- increased knowledge in the country of the usefulness of open and distance learning
- a sizeable array of existing materials, though more are needed
- an increasing amount of experience and expertise in the production and delivery of materials.

It is obviously desirable to make use of existing open/distance learning resources, particularly when they have been developed through public investment. Ideally, such materials would require clear 'quality' labelling and their appropriate credit rating. The scale of this task and its cost, for new products let alone existing ones, are high, as BAOL discovered when it considered the quality labelling of open learning materials.

There is increasingly convergence between further and higher education, particularly in professional and updating courses, and the navigation routes through materials must be clearly identifiable for learners together with appropriate guidance mechanisms.

Since a main goal of lifelong learning is to increase the nation's competitivenesss and the main area of expansion is likely to be through further education, it is not surprising that the goals of the proposed UFI are very similar both to those of the Open Tech Programme and to the Open College. The Open Tech fell down through lack of an overall framework of control. The Open College is more of a publishing house than a college, and is now clearly following a commercial route. The National Extension College is a modest analogue of the Open University operating mainly at FE and vocational level, but without adequate funding for major expansion or for social subsidy.

Neither the Open College nor the Open Tech were able or allowed to try to reach the unemployed, which the OU with its subsidised undergraduate fees and Student Hardship funds has been able to do in larger numbers. Neither have any of the structures succeeded well in reaching employees of SMEs.

The purpose of this section has been to review experience of national media-based post-school initiatives to inform a discussion about the desirability of having some national framework or organisation, using broadcasting or other appropriate telecommunications, for the delivery and support of media and technology-based open and distance learning in order to encourage access, motivation and flexibility of offering.

3 Reaching learners through institutions or learners at home

3.1 'Closed' and 'open' target groups of learners

A helpful distinction in talking about the use of the media for adult learning is to distinguish between learners in institutions, usually taught in groups or independent learners, often learning at home: either 'closed' target groups or 'open' audiences. Further and higher education and training is usually aiming at 'closed' or known target groups as distinct from broadcasting which is often speaking to an 'open' audience potentially of independent learners, College students will usually use the media offered in a 'closed' or known and controlled learning situation. The material is usually curriculum-led, and often mediated by a tutor, trainer or teacher. This is, of course, also the predominant model in schools, and may be appropriate for sections of youth and adult training. The material may be offered directly to the learner as, for example, multi-media or most broadcast programmes, or it may be designed to be mediated in some way by tutors or teachers. Schools and Open University programmes are examples of this.

Closed and Direct	**Closed and Mediated**
eg, Multi-media	eg, BBC/Channel 4 Schools, Open University
Open and Direct	**Open and Mediated**
eg, To learners direct at home	eg, To learners at home but with access to tutors eg, literacy and numeracy campaigns

Figure 6: Target groups of learners

Apart from offering the possibility of facilitation face-to-face by a tutor, institutions are also likely to be able to provide access to higher levels of technological equipment and resources than many home learners have.

Given the differing timescales for development of the new technologies and their domestic availability, it is helpful to look at options/scenarios for the short to medium term, say, three years ahead, and for the longer term (say, post-2005). Some of the issues facing institutions in particular are:

- Why is the potential of the electronic media not fully realised?
- Are we making the best use of existing resources? If not, why not?
- How do we train learners and teachers to use the technology?
- How do we help lecturers/teachers and trainers to change to become facilitators and mentors?
- What can be done to improve links between different media?
- Who is going to invest in making the programmes/software?
- How will the money flow? How can we create an efficient market? Will it be a public or private market?
- Who will own the intellectual property?
- What will be the role of public provision, public service broadcasting and libraries, and what will be private?

3.2 Horses for courses

Technology is value-free: it is simply a delivery system. One piece of technology is not intrinsically better for education or training than any other piece of technology. The question which must be asked each time is: is this the best piece of technology for the task in hand? The answer will depend on the target group, the nature of the content, the characteristics of the medium and the cost. It is vital to differentiate.

Some of the resistance to new technology has come from disappointed educators using a particular technology which was not suited to the task in view. A continuing problem has been the temptation to allow the availability of new technology to lead the project rather than the educational task. The Internet is at risk of being seen as the latest fashionable example of this tendency.

Pressure for the introduction of new technology has often come from commercial producers, both of hardware and software, or from governmental initiatives rather than from educators. There is a lot of equipment and production capacity sitting in colleges and universities which is not used effectively or enough.

3.3 Electronic/media-based learning represents a threat to the educational establishment

Educational establishments are not themselves learning but teaching institutions. Most educators have been taught face-to-face, they have been taught how to teach face-to-face, and now teach face-to-face. Many teachers are threatened by the new media as they have not been trained in its use, it denies the raison d'être of their training and may make them feel professionally inadequate. They also fear it may do them out of jobs.

Institutional structures have been created over many years to control the delivery of education and training and have held a monopoly of it. New media start to break down this monopoly. A similar process has started in broadcasting, with the disaggregation of commissioning from production and transmission, and the arrival of more choice through video, satellite and cable.

3.4 Technology does not usually function on its own

Electronically-delivered learning materials usually require some mediation. Much headway has, for example, been made in facilitating the onward educational use of broadcasting. In the educational marketplace this need will become even greater. In the US, for example, there is now a Certificate in TeleTeaching: for people who assist learners in their use of electronically-delivered education. The catch is obvious: the more personal assistance that is provided, the greater the reduction in cost-effectiveness. Using the media should not be seen as a cheap alternative to face-to-face teaching and therefore as a means of axing teachers.

3.5 Can we learn from industry?

IT and telecommunications have already had a major impact on industry. Just as the electronic office has reconfigured commerce, so it is (ultimately) likely to reconfigure education. It is this reconfiguration which is at the same time exciting and threatening.

Investment in industry is market-led. Investment in most education and training is not. The user-pays principle does not yet operate. Introducing the user-pays principle into education creates hostility, and not without some reason. We have traditionally treated education as 'free at the point of use'. To charge for it introduces a major barrier to access.

Most public sector education and training is not yet aware of the costs involved in using electronic media for education and training. This ignorance has not been helped by the strategies utilised by the private sector to encourage education into the market. For example, a commercial international database will offer a university six months' free access. After this, the institution has to start paying for the subscription, as well as for ad hoc use. More problems arise if payment is on an institution-wide basis, and the databases are more useful to some departments than others. If individual departments are paying, as they may be, for example, for satellite dishes, they may well not be prepared to let other departments in.

3.6 The ownership of intellectual property

Traditionally, academic knowledge has been in the public domain, available in research papers, journals and in books reasonably up-to-date, reasonably accessible and reasonably cheap to produce. Much new 'knowledge' is passing into the private domain, partly because research is to be funded increasingly by sponsorship from private companies and partly because of government-encouraged private investment in the ownership of intellectual property and its storage in privately owned electronic databases. Even when databases remain in public ownership, the additional cost of the electronic storage, the reception equipment and the royalty and telephone line charges becomes too high for some potential users.

Current Government policy in the UK for example, is that the delivery of training should be organised through local Training & Enterprise Councils (TECs), which are run as private companies, with boards mainly composed of local industrialists rather than educators or the public sector. This is a cause for concern as it may mean that intellectual developments in the training area also move out of the public domain into the private domain. Contracting out of training by TECs has also led to competition between private providers and local colleges for training business.

It costs money and takes time and professional expertise to develop a multi-media CD-ROM. This involves production and design expertise and commercial investment and often takes the product out of the public domain and into private ownership and control. However, a number of partnerships have been established between commercial producers and colleges and universities to develop multi-media and other learning materials, which bring together the requisite technical and learning expertise.

Broadcasters are also moving into the multi-media business, since it is often desirable to incorporate existing broadcast/video material in a multi-media project. Reports indicate that while there is a reasonable market for multi-media at school level, where the number of establishments is quite large, the market at FE level is not as developed. Of course, the use of TV material in multi-media raises copyright issues, as does the question of the ability to re-edit materials.

3.7 Increasing pressure to distinguish between open education and closed training

Increasingly some people are arguing for the proposition that 'open' education for adults should continue to go out on broadcast channels, and 'closed' education and training, which employers are prepared to pay to deliver and employees are prepared to pay to receive, can go out on subscription channels. Of course, electronic media have been employed in large organisations for much of the last two decades to deliver training. This is largely because training can be closely defined and has clear objectives which makes it suitable for electronic delivery. However, there is also only a limited amount of time on terrestrial broadcast channels which can be used to deliver education free at the point of use. Terrestrial broadcasting has been increasingly deregulated and is, as a result, increasingly competitive. There are no longer any educational obligations placed on ITV as a result of the 1990 Broadcasting Act. 'Open education for adults' is only held in place on Channel 4 and the BBC through the tradition of public-service broadcasting and its regulation.

A major concern about digital terrestrial television is that the attempt to require the 1996 Broadcasting Act to place education and other public service obligations on the new channels failed, so that there are no new educational requirements being made of digital terrestrial television, nor has the successful consortium (BDB) made any commitment to educational programming at all. This is ironic considering the all-party agreement on the importance of lifelong learning, and the additional interactive and data-broadcasting facilities which digital television will provide. There is clear evidence from North America that bespoke satellite channels for education and training are needed and used, and there is no reason why similar provision, delivered through either terrestrial or satellite broadcasting, would not be valued and effective in the UK.

Deregulation and the competition for audience ratings means that there is an increasing tendency to reduce the educational component of broadcasting, particularly difficult areas with little popular appeal. The trouble is that it is the voiceless – the poor, the unemployed, the elderly and undereducated – who are likely to rely more on broadcasting. The other important group for whom cable is not an alternative are people living in rural areas. The responsibility for providing such broadcasting should be made clear by Parliament. The user-pays principle is not appropriate.

3.8 Why is the potential of educational broadcasting and other electronic media not realised?

Not enough is known about the effectiveness of educational television. This is ridiculous since many appropriate research techniques are available and are in regular use for measuring the effectiveness of advertising. It has been suggested that 'little attention had *ever* been paid to its effectiveness because it has no price tag attached to it!' There could and should be high quality research carried out to demonstrate its real effectiveness. However, some cynics have argued, such research will only be commissioned when there is a real market in educational provision and people are paying for it directly.

Industry, in particular, would like to know how the different technologies work, for what purposes, at what costs. Of course, further and higher education also need to know this! Will, for example, an electronic campus be cost-effective? Will student residences need to be wired? Do all people learn equally from different media?

3.9 What are the forces for change?

The learners of the future will be a great force for change. Children are already growing up in an electronic-rich environment at home. It is children who programme videos, play computer games, have computer smartcards. Forty-five per cent of large families with children now own personal computers. It is parents and teachers who lag behind and lack confidence.

The problem with the education industry is that it has been isolated from telematic changes in industry and from the outside world. It has also been starved by Government of funds for such developments. Many teachers have therefore been cut off from today's technology and reject it because they are fearful of it. Recent research shows many FE teachers without a PC on their desk or easily available to them. The OU did not make a breakthrough with its staff using new technology until it had 'one (ie, a PC) on every desk'. It is encouraging that *The Learning Divide* shows computer studies as top of the subjects being studied by adults, among older as well as younger age-groups.

Multi-media PCs are increasingly being bought for home use, especially for large adult households and large households with children. However, while sales are increasing, the trends shown in Figures 7 and 8 indicate that some of it is a replacement market and that the proportions of older people and younger people living alone with PCs are surprisingly low.

It is therefore important to be reminded about the current level of availability of such equipment in people's homes. The assumption that such equipment is already available to most people is not correct. Figure 7 records the increase in ownership of TV sets, videos, phones and PCs over the last decade, showing effective saturation for TV and telephone but not for video and with quite low ownership still for PCs. At the same time, it is likely, given the trends, that ownership among large families has reached 50% by now.

	TV	Phone	Video	PC
1985	98	81	31	13
1989	98	87	60	19
1991	98	88	68	21
1993	98	90	73	24
1994	99	91	77	24
1995	99	93	79	25

Figure 7: Ownership by households (%) of TV set, video, phone and PC

	TV	Phone	Video	PC
1 person, age 16–59	95	82	70	19
2 people, age 16–59	99	95	92	32
1 person, 60+	98	90	35	2
2 people, ½ 60+	100	98	76	10
Small family	99	93	94	36
Large family	99	88	93	45
Large adult family	99	98	94	43
All households	99	93	79	25

Figure 8: Ownership by household type (%) 1995

3.10 Changes in structures of further and higher education

The breakdown of the traditional vertically integrated degree and qualification structure into credits and other smaller modules with Credit Accumulation and Transfer schemes encourages the use of a variety of flexible learning resources in mixed modes of study. Different electronic media can be selected for specific teaching purposes, as well as providing learners with a choice of methods of study. The move to a unified framework of post-school qualifications will encourage this further. And communications technologies will play a critical role in facilitating these processes in the interests of learners.

3.11 Changing learners

More learners will be adults studying part-time, fitting their studies in with their lives and work. Students will vote with their feet, choosing flexibility and openness. It will be essential for further education to be organised in such a way that people can keep their jobs and carry on learning at the same time. Constant retraining will become a fact of life: it will need to be 'hassle-free' and treated as an automatic part of human resource development.

If media-based education can be used to deliver part-time opportunities all over the country, without extra financial barriers, it will also help redress the urban/metropolitan bias in further education.

3.12 Changing funding mechanisms

Increasingly funding will not go to institutions as such: it will either be directed at the technologies or at the learners. High tech companies will put money into the technologies which most easily win user support and facilitate learning.

Employers are also likely to support 'open and distance learning' for their employees. Development work by the MSC/Training Agency over the years has increased knowledge and acceptance of open and resource-based learning in industry.

Funding may also go directly to learners in the form of training credits or educational entitlements. Learners will then choose to use their credits on what is convenient for them. User-pays would also become a decisive element in a broadcast system that had to be self-financed, for example, digital satellite.

3.13 Who will fund the development of the software?

What counts in electronic education is the software or courseware. This is what the learner sees and interacts with. However, the potential for learning of the hardware has almost always been in advance of the design of the software. The hardware provides new facilities which need to be exploited to aid learning, but there is little point in people buying expensive PCs if there is little appropriate software. CD-ROMs are currently at this critical stage of development, an important point since CD-ROMs look like being particularly useful for educators and trainers since it is possible to store TV and video material as well as sound, stills and text on the same disc, and also provide some interactivity.

There is not, however, enough high quality educational software or courseware packages on the market to help create a large enough demand for the new hardware, and therefore bring the price of the hardware down to a domestic level. Effort is now concentrating on developing software, but who will invest in it and who will own it? The development of edutainment is expected to help to stimulate the market, and multi-media computers are certainly being bought for the home. This could have a beneficial effect on the development of multi-media products for education and lifelong learning.

The OU has, until recently, worked on the principle that as a distance learning institution delivering to people's homes it cannot be too far ahead of what is happening in the domestic market. It can be *slightly* ahead, but not *well* ahead. Conventional institutions can be *well* ahead because they are dealing with students in an institutional environment. The OU's initial computer scheme in the 70s had to be funded to assist students to acquire computers. At the moment conventional institutions do not (yet) require students to have their own computers, though this option is now being discussed by some. More recently, the OU has decided that for some courses it is reasonable to require high-grade PC ownership, accepting that this may cost £1,000 or more. There is depressing evidence that, as a result of the increased new technology demands, the proportion of women enrolling on the Technology Foundation Course has dropped dramatically.

3.14 The desk-top university, the electronic work-station, the wired class-room and the global electronic village

It will not be long before learning is regularly delivered to the desk-top, whether this is at home or at work. The higher up the academic level, the nearer one is to the reality of the global electronic village. Learning can already be delivered at the desk-top, whether at home or at work. Many universities and colleges are finally starting to move away from lecturers reading out from notes as a form of information delivery. A number are already setting up information networks. Heriot-Watt, for example, is linking up student accommodation with an electronic network system. Scotland is doing interesting work with electronic media and open and distance learning partly stimulated by the demands imposed by an isolated and scattered population and a University of the Highlands and Islands is being set up.

One of the most exciting developments in training is that of interactive workstations. Managements are investing in the idea because it saves money. It is cheaper to train people through interactive videos and electronic networks than to bring people together from all over the country, let alone from over Europe. However, while private companies are investing in multi-media and workstations, most colleges will find the costs high.

The Commonwealth of Learning and a European Open University are all moves in this direction. The OU increasingly sees itself as having a worldwide rather than a UK role. Certainly this includes Eastern Europe, where English is acceptable as a language for instruction. At this stage there is a role for trans-frontier satellite provision. Again, who pays?

4 Media strategies

4.1 Media technologies available for delivery

Despite the hype in the newspapers and the special supplements, the latest sophisticated technology – multi-media, broad-band, cable, the Internet – are in mass learning terms still in their infancy. BT's recent report *Listening to the Nation* records the majority of personal communication as still face-to-face (86%), with 12% by telephone and 2% by letter. Less than 0.5%, they note, is by fax or E-mail, 'although almost everyone believes the ability to communicate by computer will become more important over the next ten years'. (BT,1997) In the shorter term, if wider access and participation is the goal, and we wish to reach new groups of people, including ethnic minorities, women returners, people in rural areas, the unemployed, as well people in small businesses, many of whom will want or need to learn at home, then it is sensible to use the technology which is already widely available in people's homes and at reasonable cost, rather than leap-frogging to the more sophisticated technology.

This strategy does not, of course, rule out a complementary strategy, suggested by commercial interests, which could, in addition, be used to deliver access to more sophisticated technology through cable or ISDN lines, etc, to colleges and other community sites eg, public libraries and community centres. It is likely that major advances of this nature will involve and benefit from cross-sectoral public/private finance initiatives.

4.2 What is an optimum technology strategy for a new nationally linked initiative?

It has been suggested in relation to the suggested UFI (Harris, 1995) that a new national project need nowadays not depend on any one particular delivery mechanism, but on appropriate organisational and contractual linkages and innovations. The analysis of the histories of previous projects discussed earlier confirms this approach. It is unlikely, for example, that a vertically integrated production-led total institution in the mould of the BBC or the OU would provide the required flexibility.

Increasingly many vertically-integrated large institutions are being down-sized and disaggregated or deconstructed into their component functions, with some functions being delivered through sub-contracting or out-sourcing. The comparison that has been made is with Channel 4, which commissions and quality controls the financing and production of programmes but does not produce them.

A new initiative, Harris notes, could treat technology in one of three ways:

1. It could regard a particular advanced technological solution eg, broadband cable as the fundamental basis of the project.
2. The project could be established and run *independently* of technology, as the Open College and the OLF are.
3. It could use whatever technology was appropriate, in line with evolving institutional needs; effectively the current OU strategy.

Despite continued suggestions, the cost, lack of universality and roll-out time of broadband cable implicit in Option 1 does not recommend it as a national strategy for FE colleges. Option 2 is too negative and backward-looking. Option 3 would allow a choice of existing low tech technologies such as TV, video and audio to be used as well as new multi-media and networking technologies where appropriate.

4.3 Who pays and at what point in the process for these services?

4.3.1 Broadcasting

Until now, most post-school education, and of course the BBC, have been free at the point of use and paid for by the 'community' through taxation and the licence fee. The strength of broadcasting for the OU as it began was that the television programmes were delivered free to the learner at home, nearly universally over all the country. Though few OU programmes are now watched live, broadcasting still provides a very cheap delivery system for learners who record programmes for later viewing.

It has been vital for the OU over the years to work at the level of the domestic market, with equipment that most people already have at home e.g. TV, radio, audio and video-recorders and telephone. This has decreased the need for new funding and has assisted in learner access.

4.3.2 The Internet

Increasingly and particularly with new technologies, costs are being shifted directly to users. Newer technologies are not cheap to the user at home, and the direct cost is usually concealed from individual users in companies or universities as it not borne by the individual user. Much current access to the Internet, for example, is at the workplace or university. At home it requires a high-grade PC, a phone line (two for frequent users) and a modem, with little change from £1000.

The Internet essentially does two things: it acts as a large library, a marvellous browserie for those with enough time, and it enables asynchronous electronic messages (E-Mail) between individuals and groups over much of the world. For all the hype, the current Internet use is low and access is highly work-related. A recent survey by Continental Research (ITC,1995) showed high awareness of it (68% claiming to be aware, rising to 78% in London). More men than women were aware (76% vs 60%) and more managers/professionals then manual workers (88% vs 47%) and more young than old (76% of 15-24s vs 40% of over-64-year-olds. However, only 6.9% claimed to have access to the NET, and this was mainly at work. The research suggests that around 1 million have access at home.

The Internet will not provide instant miracles for learners. While there are some educational courses and resources already available and being experimented with on the Internet, it is expensive to prepare them for entry in an appropriate form, and not easy to see why people should do it 'philanthropically'. There is also an issue of intellectual property and cost recovery.

What it is excellent for is bringing together groups of people who are scattered but who share a common interest: Internet tutorials for distance learning, self-help study groups, virtual study circles. It enable virtual course-teams to work together and specialists to confer with each other. It will increasingly enable the preparation and use of bottom-up learner-friendly resource materials, where ownership, plagiarism, copyright and standards are not issues.

4.3.3 Cable

Apart from its cost, cable will never be universally available: about 15% of the population will never be covered. And where franchises have been let, the progress being made in digging up the roads is still very slow, and the rate of signing-up is low: of the 6.4 million broadband homes passed by January 1 1996, only 1.4 million homes were connected. The average rate of connection is running at 22%. Telephony has provided an additional stimulus to its marketing: 97 out of 105 companies are offering telephony services and the proportion taking up these services is over 90%. (ITC,1996)

4.3.4 BBC's The Learning Zone

The BBC started using its night-time hours for a specialist education and training service under the name BBC Select, designed to deliver programmes to specialist audiences such as nurses, lawyers and the voluntary sector. It has now extended its night-time service, renamed *The Learning Zone*, to transmit a wider range of educational programming, including a bespoke service for further education and some BBC Schools and OU repeats. This is proving very valuable for motivated and organised learners with video-recorders, both individuals and groups. However, night-time transmissions are effectively out of sight and therefore much less suitable for unmotivated groups who do not yet know what they want or are interested in.

4.3.5 Digital terrestrial services

There had been optimism that the new digital terrestrial television channels would provide new opportunities for educational programming and experimentation with interactivity. Two and a half multiplexes have been allocated to current analogue broadcasters to enable them to simulcast their existing services. It is likely that the BBC will add some educational services, using the sidechannels on its own multiplex. However, as of now, Channel 4 and ITV are not promising any additional services and the three new multiplex services have been let to a consortium, BDB, which has made no educational commitments at all. Their licences are to be granted for 12 years in the first instance, with a further 12 years renewable. Digital will also require set-top boxes, incurring an additional cost. What has also been conceded is that in the event of an early withdrawal of analogue services, current education and public service obligations will be transferred to the appropriate digital services.

The point at issue is that there is no current proposal to enable education and training to benefit from the extension of choice and provision offered by the arrival of digital broadcast technology. Education and training require a service which delivers free at the point of use, not one to be paid for directly by the learner.

It is disgraceful that a nation committed to the achievement of ambitious targets for Education and Training (NTETs) could fail to make the connection between these goals and the use of the new digital terrestrial opportunities for adult learning. The US now has several education and training channels available. The suggestion that one channel should be earmarked for an education and training channel is obvious common sense. It is important that some education/training obligation is placed on the new publicly-regulated channels, whether across the board or through the allocation of a specific educational/training channel. A bespoke channel could be run as a non-profit consortium offering space to a number of providers, an FE network, the National Extension College and the Open College. The proposed UFI might also be a user of such a specific channel.

4.4 Telecommunications

Telecommunications will become an increasingly important player. ISDN lines, though not particularly cheap, will enable delivery through libraries, open learning or community centres and may provide a universally available option. However, the timetable of its roll-out is not clear. The OFTEL consultation paper *Universal Telecommunications Services* (OFTEL, 1996) asked what a universal service for telecommunications means. It notes that 'the principle of everyone having access to the communications networks of the day has been a fundamental goal of successful economies throughout history. . . . Today, basic service means access to digital networks'.

> *The most important objective is to ensure that customers throughout the country have universal access to a reasonably affordable basic telecommunications service at an appropriate level of capability.*

It put forward arrangements for funding and delivering universal service across the industry which are *'fair and transparent, and which encourage competitive delivery by the market wherever possible'.*

The three policy principles spelled out were:

geographic accessibility – access to the same service on the same terms throughout the UK.
affordability – services at tariffs that customers can reasonably afford.
equal opportunities – opportunities for customers with special needs to have reasonable access to services.

It added that certain categories of customer, such as people with disabilities, schools or public libraries, may need to access a different level of service at appropriate rates throughout the UK. 'OFTEL therefore believes that it is appropriate to seek to define universal service levels for specific customer groups, in order to achieve wider economic and social policy goals.'

The 1996 OFTEL paper took a narrow definition of education institutions and focused on schools for 5-16-year-olds. The case was therefore made to OFTEL by NIACE that adult education institutions and colleges and other public sites needed to be added to the list. The follow-up report of their *Education and Public Access Points Task Force* (OFTEL,1997) is helpful in that it has 'focused on the telecommunications needs of schools and the FE sector as well as public libraries' though it is not possible to review the detail of its recommendations in this paper.

It did not consider the needs of the higher education sector as 'it was considered to be relatively well catered for in terms of network connectivity by the JANET and SUPERJANET Network'. Neither did it consider the needs of adult education centres outside of the FE sector. An interesting issue is how far JANET and SUPERJANET could or should also be accessible outside the walls of their institutions: electronic extra-mural departments, as it were.

Another possibility worth testing is whether or not 'registered open/distance learners' could form a class of customer at a special tariff. Since increasingly adults study part-time, are often home/workplace-based and are enabled to do so by technology, it is somewhat perverse for them only to have access to a special tariff by physically going to the institution that arranges their learning, when the very technology enables them not to have to do that.

4.5 What would telematics deliver?

The convergence of telecommunications, computing and television, referred to increasingly as telematics, provides new opportunities for reaching and supporting learners. Available for this task is a combination of computing technology, enabling interactive computing, and communications technology, enabling networking, which *together* provide the potential to create systems which can deliver self-paced, tutor-supported learning over a distance.

It is, of course, possible simply to transmit basic face-to-face class-room teaching using ISDN lines and similarly to transmit the text of lectures / teaching notes or other materials by computer, E-Mail or other media, eg, audio, video or CD-Rom. This may or may not be cheaper than using time-honoured print and post. At minimum, the simple transfer of linear text-based courses is likely to need to include the preparation of an index, a guide to internal navigation, a dictionary/ glossary and assessment tests, with probably the addition of a tutor's guide to its teaching methodology. The text itself needs to be keyed in, or scanned, at some cost.

Distance education means literally that the teacher is at a distance from the learner. This requires the careful preparation of materials designed for the learner to learn independently of direct contact with the teacher. The learner will initiate and control learning. It is, in the jargon, learner-centred.

With multi-media, the teacher becomes the 'supporter of self-paced learning'. The learning is asynchronous and aspatial. It is necessary to structure the knowledge to facilitate learning, to help the learner manage the interaction with the knowledge. There is much current interest in multi-media formats since they are seen to provide the possibility of greater interaction for the learner with the learning materials. They are particularly suitable for courses where the academic content is not linear, where there is cross-indexing, with a variety of course inputs/materials and multiple random interactions. They are, however, not cheap to prepare.

At the same time, research indicates that the freedom to roam and question provided by random access multi-media formats may bring with it problems. The key characteristic of broadcast television, as with books, is its narrative structure. This structure provides a helpful guide to the learner, particularly to learners who are new to the area and may be less than confident in their knowledge. The warning in Laurillard's ESRC research proposal is clear, that the lack of structure in multi-media may be a disadvantage to some, probably weaker, students.

> *For interactive media, one of the key benefits is seen as being the lack of imposed structure, giving much greater freedom of control to the user. However, in the context of instruction this benefit runs counter to the learner's need to discern structure if there is a message to be understood.*
>
> *We have found from observation that learners working on interactive media with no clear narrative structure display learning behaviour that is generally unfocused and inconclusive . . . Thus one of the key benefits of interactive media, the greater learner control it offers, becomes pedagogically disadvantageous if it results in mere absence of structure.* (Laurillard et al, 1995)

4.6 Interactivity

Interactivity is talked about a lot. It has always been a main rationale for face-to-face contact. Many teachers have been particularly concerned to provide for interactivity for learners and between groups of learners. Much technological interactivity has so far been achieved through teleconferencing clamped onto satellite broadcasting, that is one-way video, two-way audio. ISDN lines already allow for limited quality two-way video. The combination of cable and ISDN lines will allow individual interactivity. CD-I and related developments start to combine the delivery of centrally-produced multi-media resources with the capacity of individual interactivity, though its development costs are still high. Independent learning requires the building of interactivity into the learning materials from the outset, either into the printed course materials or into the multi-media disk.

In discussing interactivity, it is helpful to separate the notion of interaction between the content and the learner, from that between the tutor and the learner (or groups of learners) and, thirdly, interactions between learners themselves, for examples in study circles or self-help groups.

It is not yet clear whether it is the personalisation of the message, the interactivity inside the content, the interactivity with the tutor, or with other students that is more important for learners. It is likely to differ for different learners or for different courses. Different subject areas are likely to support varying depths and degrees of interactivity. More work is needed on 'how much/what depth of interactivity?', 'for what types of content?', 'for whom?', and 'at what cost?' since the cost of developing pathways of multi-media activity is great and may not be justified if its provision only meets the need of small numbers.

To answer these questions is extremely important since the time and money that may be invested in producing CD-Roms, for example, is great. There are many subject areas, particularly suitable for CD-Rom, where there is a large amount of basic reference material to which local learners will not have easy access. This can include stills, moving images, voice and text. A serious issue with these new forms which draw on existing materials from different media is the issue of copyright and the ownership of intellectual property. This is a major issue currently with the Internet. Many people are busy trying to work out how to make money out of the Internet, and education is not likely to be exempt from this tendency. Figure 9 lists the main available technologies, with an indication of their availability.

Type	Available to home	Equipment cost/availability
Terrestrial broadcasting	Free/universal	TV set Video recorder
Narrowcasting on broadcast channels e.g. Learning Zone	Free/universal	Decoder option
Satellite	Subscription/Universal signal	Dish
Cable/satellite into cable heads	Subscription/Cable areas only	Cable to home Control unit
Via telephone lines:		
Internet	Via phone line(s)	Phone/extra line PC Modem
ISDN lines	New ISDN line(s)	Cost
Video on demand	Via phone line/TV	Control box
Multi-media	PC/software	Computer
CD-rom, CD-I	Cost of CDs	CD player/drive
DVD	Future availability is uncertain	

Figure 9: Delivery systems

4.7 Why not use a satellite channel?

Why is the UK so far behind North America in its use of satellites to deliver education and training to colleges, homes and to the workplace? In the US many companies use satellites to train their staff, for teleconferencing and for in-house communications to other sites. There is a whole industry of journals, professional associations and databases providing information about business television, teleconferencing and distance learning. Many colleges and universities offer distance learning courses via satellite on linked or franchise sites. Of course the US has a lighter regulatory regime and stronger geographical imperatives to use satellites than the UK.

Similarly, the UK Employment Department-funded Starnet project using Olympus concluded that corporate training, professional updating and teleconferencing were likely to be the most appropriate models for satellite-delivered education and training.

The advantage of satellite is that its signal is universal, that the cost of dishes is low and dropping. Using a satellite (or two) to reach a motivated audience, whether in a network of colleges, at home or at the workplace, is a realistic proposition. It is also possible to serve such special needs groups as the deaf and hard of hearing. One commercial provider in the US is already filling four transponders with commercial training materials eg, for fire prevention and law enforcement officers.

Digital satellite is set to arrive in the UK within the year, earlier than digital terrestrial, bringing an explosion in the quantity of available channels by a factor of 10, and with it inevitably at some point a consequent reduction in price. While new set-top boxes will not be very cheap, they are likely to become cheaper and should be usable on both terrestrial and satellite systems. They will certainly be within the budget of colleges even if not immediately of individuals.

It is noteworthy that the recent EBU feasibility study for a European Educational Channel concluded that digital satellite was likely to offer the most appropriate delivery system. (Gwynne-Jones and Hasebrinck,1995)

Issues of conditional access are relevant both to digital terrestrial and to digital satellite broadcasts. What is vital is that set-top boxes are designed with a common interface to permit the receipt of 'free-to-air services'.

4.8 What could a satellite usefully deliver?

4.8.1 Traditional broadcast quality programmes

The UK education/training tradition in broadcasting has been to prepare carefully crafted programmes in the mould of BBC/public service broadcasting. These are very expensive to make but reach a large audience and once made can continue to serve large numbers of people through repeats or video. There is some existing programme material of this sort such as OU and schools programmes which the BBC are using for their night-time service, *The Learning Zone*.

4.8.2 (Live) transmission of lectures/classes to remote sites

Satellites are also used widely in America to transmit lectures and tutorials to classes in several locations with students able to respond live by phone/satellite. This could be useful for colleges franchising to other sites or delivering to home learners. It is also valuable for companies with several sites. Microwave and ISDN lines can be used in the same way.

4.8.3 A materials distribution system

Another valuable use is as a Resource Materials Distribution Service to colleges and their learning centres, and indeed to individuals. Its data broadcasting capacity is increasingly important as is its facility for networking for both students and tutors.

4.8.4 Interactivity through satellite

As noted earlier, much interactivity has so far been achieved through tele or audio conferencing clamped on to satellite broadcasting ie, one-way video, two-way audio. The addition of data-broadcasting and asynchronous teleconferencing again combines the delivery of centrally produced multi-media resources with the capacity of offering individual and group interactivity, though it is not necessarily cheap.

4.8.5 The National Technological University and other US models

There is no reason except habit and expectation why a satellite channel cannot carry a variety of types of educational offerings, from pre-prepared conventional broadcast programmes to modest-cost lecture series or lab demonstrations to simple talking-head tutorials with phone-ins.

There is, however, a clear difference between an OU-type course model which prepares a fully structured integrated media-based distance learning course for delivery with an amount of planned tutor contact and other complementary learning support and a conventional course that is simply offered to a larger number of people by transmitting it live or pre-recorded in the same way to other groups of students as if the students were in the same class-room – a virtual class-room, as it were.

There are a number of interesting models in the US. *The National Technological University* (NTU) offers a wide range of instructional television courses via satellite taught by the top faculty of 46 leading engineering universities. Each participating university that delivers courses has an earth station or uplink. NTU is accredited by the appropriate Commission on Institutions of Higher Education. NTU also allows course exchange between participating NTU institutions using each other's courses under agreed financial and academic arrangements.

The *Mind Extension University* (MEU) and the Public Broadcasting Service (PBS) *Adult Learning Service* (ALS) work somewhat differently. If the OU is likened to Sainsbury, as a mass provider of high quality goods for which Sainsbury is centrally responsible, MEU and the ALS are more like SPAR, the grocery network. MEU operates as a 'front-of-house operation' controlling the interface with the learners but behind this is a deal with the supplying institutions: over content, publishing, taught content, support and accreditation. MEU uses other people's programmes, but also makes its own. It has a very clear front-of-house operation with a toll-free number, an easy-to-tune-to satellite service. It is good for learners, because it is 'one-trip'. It is good for providers, because it brings learners in on a sensible basis.

The ALS provides telecourses delivered by satellite combining TV programmes, tutor guides and learner guides, usually accredited for bachelor or associate degrees. Tuition and assessment is offered by community colleges who pay a royalty per registered student to ALS centrally, thus contributing to the overall marketing and development of new courses.

It is possible to envisage a similar arrangement here whereby a non-profit consortium could run a satellite channel for an FE network and offer a deal to colleges and TECs which helped them reach more people, reaching beyond their existing boundaries with the colleges/TECs/companies providing the materials and the delivery consortium offering the economies of scale. There is also no reason why a number of different strategies should not be adopted if they are appropriate and cost-effective.

A major concern is that the MEU and others are already moving into the UK and into Europe, and unless the UK makes progress with local provision they may increasingly dominate the market.

4.9 Other uses for new technologies

The use of the media for course delivery is only part of the story. Any new network or consortium will be heavily dependent on technology for the spine of its whole operation: for building up a database of approved course materials, for the delivery of advice and guidance, the recording of individual learning plans (and maybe learning accounts), for correspondence tutoring, the provision of learning support, for linking networks of tutors and students.

A particular need will be a student progress and tracking system, which allows learners to build up a record of achievement, a learning passport, and which could form the basis of a unified credit accumulation and transfer system over post-school education.

4.10 Who pays: consumer rights and consumer protection

The increasing shift of payment by the community to payments by adults and employers for their learning brings a new barrier to access to learning, and the financing of disadvantaged learners becomes an even more difficult issue. It also raises issues of consumer rights and consumer protection.

It is clear that new technologies will deliver much new content and provide new opportunities for adult learning. What is less clear is how adults will navigate their ways through these new opportunities. Several things will happen. Adults will choose for themselves how and what they wish to learn but increasingly they will pay, or will pay a greater share of, the costs of their learning. They will need more information and guidance and learning support through that learning. These will not necessarily be provided in time-honoured ways: electronic communication in one form or another is likely to become increasingly important.

As learners pay directly for themselves, there will be more pressure for education to be looked on as a consumer good, indeed as a business and consumer principles and accountability come into play. It was matching the HUNT plans for cable against the National Consumer Council's (NCC) set of basic consumer principles which made it clear that cable as it was then being planned could not be expected to meet consumers' needs, let alone educators' needs. (McIntosh,1982) The basic principles the NCC has identified if people's needs as consumers are to be met are a) access and availability; b) information; c) choice; d) value for money; e) redress for consumers; f) representation. All of these requirements apply to education: adequate and clear information that is user-friendly, alternative forms of supply, reasonable class times, avoidance of geographical barriers, clear information about value for money, complaints and redress machinery. Unlike most nationalised and some newly-privatised industries there is no adequate complaints machinery for education. And consumer representation in education is patchy.

As courses are delivered in smaller units, and are individually developed and costed, it will be increasingly necessary for learners to know what they are paying for and whether it is appropriate to their learning needs. The implication is that the entry behaviour expected for a particular module will need to be clear, together ideally with a diagnostic test to check on readiness. The level of the test will marry back to the preceding module, another task for new technologies! Such issues are starting to be touched on in the increased emphasis on quality, and are implicit in the Citizen's Charter and in Learners' Charters.

Finally, the serious challenge is to use the new technologies to extend opportunity and not to exclude more people – to bring more people into the information society, not to make more of them information-poor.

References

ACACE. (1982) *Continuing Education: from policies to practice.* Leicester: ACACE

Ainley, P. & Corney, M. (1990) *Training for the future.* London: Cassell Educational Ltd

Ansoff, H.I.(1965) *Corporate Strategy.* New York: McGraw-Hill

Birnbaum, N. (1974) 'A view from New England' In *The Open University Opens.* Tunstall, J. London: Routledge, Kegan Paul

Colenso, M. (1995) Personal communication.

EC. (1991) *Open Distance learning,* Com (91). 388 Brussels

Fulton, O. (1981) *Access to higher education.* Guildford: Society for Research into Higher Education

Groombridge, B. (1996) 'Broadcasting and adult education' In *A history of modern British adult education.* Fieldhouse, R. Leicester: NIACE

Hasebrinck,U. & Gwynne-Jones,E. (1995) *European Educational television: a feasibility study.* Hamburg: Hans-Bredow-Institute

HMSO. (1969) *Report of the Planning Committee for the Open University to the Secretary of State for Education and Science.* London: HMSO

Laurillard, D. et al (1995) *Multi-media, education and narrative organisation* – ESRC proposal In mimeograph. Milton Keynes: Open University

Lewis,R. & McDonald,L. (1988) *The Open Learning Pocket Book.* NCET

McIntosh, N. (1971) *'Knowledge and awareness of the Open University. In mimeograph'.* Milton Keynes: Open University

McIntosh, N. (1983) *How will information technology serve the community?* London: PITCOM 1 2

MSC. (1981) *An 'Open Tech' programme.* London: MSC

MSC. (1982) *'Open Tech' Task Group Report.* Sheffield: MSC

Murdoch,R. (1989) *Freedom in broadcasting* The MacTaggart Lecture, Edinburgh International Television Festival 25.08.1989. NP: News Corporation Ltd

OFTEL. (1995) *Universal Telecommunications Services.* London: OFTEL

OFTEL. (1997) *Information highways: improving access for school colleges and public information points.* London: OFTEL

Sargant, N. (1990)* 'Access and the media' In *Access and alternative futures for higher education.* Ed. Parry, G. and Wake, C. London: Hodder & Stoughton

Sargant, N. (1991)* 'An Open Polytechnic to complement the UKOU?' In *La educacion no formal, una prioridad de futuro.* Madrid: Fundacion Santillana

Sargant, N. (1991)* 'Choosing to use the media' In *The BUFVC handbook for film and television in education.* London: BUFVC

Sargant, N. (1992)* Report of the working parting on higher and further education and training. In mimeograph and summarised in *Electronic Education: its role in a learning society.* London: Royal Society of Arts

Sargant, N. (1992)* *Adult learners, broadcasting and Channel 4.* London: Channel 4/Broadcasting Support Services

Sargant, N. (1996)* 'The University for Industry: what can we learn from other initiatives?' Paper prepared for IPPR seminar. In mimeograph.

Sargant, N. (1996)* 'The University for Industry: the medium is not the message. Paper prepared for IPPR seminar. In mimeograph.

Sargant, N. (1997)* Broadcasting and the adult learner – a review of current research and research needs' In *Educational television – what do people want?.* IZI Munich/University of Luton Press

Sargant, N. (1997)* 'Technology and adult learners' In *Adults Learning Vol 9 No 1.* Leicester: NIACE

Sargant, N. (1997)* 'The Open University' In *A history of modern British adult education.* Ed. Fieldhouse, R. Leicester: NIACE

Tuckett, A. (1997) *Motivation is Curriculum.* (In print) Leicester: NIACE

UDACE. (1988) *Developing Access.* Leicester: UDACE

Yeats, C. A. (1986) *The teaching of science and technology at a distance.* MA dissertation. University of London

Motivation Is Curriculum

Introduction

Most of our education and training structures, our buildings and timetables have been designed with the young in mind. Many adults adapt to make use of them, but many are put off and most simply never consider the question. Provision for adults needs recruitment and retention to be recognised as key dimensions in the curriculum, since unless adults can be encouraged to participate, there is no curriculum discussion to be had. For that reason, 'who participates' is the key question for further education.

The FEFC's Widening Participation Committee has a refreshingly open brief. In seeking to extend participation in further education to groups of young people and adults currently under-represented among its student cohort, it must inevitably look at how demand can be stimulated.

This paper argues that for a responsive further education system motivation is curriculum, that there are a set of educational skills in negotiating appropriate programmes of learning for young people and adults returning to education so that it is a new and exciting experience rather than a return to the scene of disappointment and failure. It argues that there are important alliances to be fostered with local, regional and national media which are the natural channels of communication for some of these groups. It makes recommendations to the Widening Participation Committee that the FEFC should dedicate resources to stimulating demand at a national level; that it should foster alliances to the same end in its regions, and that colleges should collaborate at a local level with other providers to create the conditions for widened participation.

Practical Collaboration

Broadcasting

Education has been a core activity for broadcasters from the beginning – since the BBC's charter identified disseminating 'information, education and entertainment' as its core function (HMSO, 1926). Radio and television have a major impact on most of our lives – shaping the agenda of public debate, informing our roles as active citizens, stimulating curiosity and, occasionally, teaching. As Lady Plowden remarked, memorably, 'Broadcasting is democratic – there are no reserved seats'. (Plowden, 1980)

As Naomi Sargant argues, television is free at the point of use, reaches people in their own homes, and has a greater reach than any other education and training medium. (Sargant, 1992) Will Hutton summarised the strengths and limitations of the medium for securing informed debate, at a BBC Conference on Broadcasting and the Learning Society in 1991:

> 'Television's great advantage is the ability to reduce highly complex subjects to a level of simplicity understandable by mass audiences. The ability to combine the graphic and visual elements with words that reinforce the picture gives television its powerful intellectual force. . . For full effect, television programmes need to be built on. We should be wary about the effects of the first hit. I'm also wary about the amount of information television can actually get across. Another problem is that television is not really allowed to come of age. In writing an article, I can be objective while making comments of my

own. Television and radio producers are not allowed to own a view, or to argue a partial position, and this leads to a certain blandness of much of what we watch.' (Hutton, 1991)

Most of the public attention to learning and the media has focused on the work of the media in and for the direct delivery of planned educational programmes. However, the focus of this paper is on the use of the media to arouse curiosity, to give the confidence and the motivation for people to find out more, and to participate in learning activities. There is a substantial body of experience in the last 20 years which shows that alliances between broadcasters and providers succeed in stimulating participation among under-represented groups.

Adult Literacy Campaign

The decision by the BBC to mount a high-profile campaign encouraging people with reading and writing problems to seek help from the education and training system transformed public provision in 1975. The BBC decision was taken in 1971/2, and the programming agreed involved a melange of 10-minute sketches in peak viewing time, and included documentary witness slots ('I was an adult illiterate'), authoritative discussion about language, and elegant graphics. It made Bob Hoskins a star, but more importantly (for further education at least) it established the power of television in motivating non-participating adults to join in. The programmes went out on the mass market channel, BBC1, at tea-times on Sunday, backed by sessions for tutors on BBC2, and on radio. High quality support materials and a free telephone referral service were also provided.

At the same time as the BBC was deciding to mount *On The Move*, the British Association of Settlements co-ordinated an Adult Literacy Campaign which culminated in the Ministerial decision to divert £1 million of the universities' top-up money in 1975 to fund an Adult Literacy Resource Agency through the then National Institute of Adult Education, NIACE's predecessor. It is a feature of the times that the universities never noticed the loss of the budget. The tenacity of the Campaign and the importance of the issue have ensured that there has been a national agency, now called the Basic Skills Agency, and steadily increasing levels of public investment ever since. Almost overnight the literacy campaign led to an increase in student numbers from 6,000 to 60,000, and then 100,000. Thousands more people contacted the helpline to volunteer as tutors.

The literacy campaign established that such collaborations between broadcasters and local providers could reveal previously unexpressed demand. It spawned many later imitators, and the creation of the voluntary organisation, Broadcasting Support Services, which provides a wide variety of follow-up and back-up materials to programmes, including, increasingly, telephone helpline services. For the first time in the UK, an educational programme which addressed the system's failures was backed with high production values and quality support materials, previously limited to elite studies. As a result adult literacy provision was developed, and continues to enjoy positive public and political support.

Numeracy

Yorkshire Television followed up the broadcasting-led literacy campaign with *Make It Count* in 1977 and *Numbers at Work* – two series seeking to use television to help people who find numbers incomprehensible. Pro-rata the response to the programmes on ITV was impressive – yet overall the numeracy initiative produced a smaller response than the literacy campaign. It was, interestingly, updated and repeated on Channel 4 with a third series added, and then used several years running. 40,000 people requested the workbook that the National Extension College produced as back-up to the programmes and the audience, small for television, averaged 423,000 at first showing on Channel 4 and 127,000 on repeat. (NEC, 1983) The series was innovative in producing early experiments linking Channel 4 and the NEC in offering computerised individual feedback to learners studying the workbook.

Women returners

Until the 1990 Broadcasting Act was passed, independent television companies had a legal duty to show educational programmes for adults, as did the BBC and Channel 4. Much of the regional programming was in what became known as social action broadcasting, linking broadcasts, informal learning, and issues of local, topical concern. However, the Independent Broadcasting Authority (IBA), and later the Independent Television Commission (ITC), ensured that nationally networked educational programmes were also scheduled. There were, of course, inevitable tensions between the aspirations of programme controllers seeking the flexibility to maximise audience and those of the IBA/ITC. The commercial companies lobbied to secure a relaxation to the regulatory obligations to preserve educational programmes in mass audience evening slots, and in the run-up to the 1990 Act decided to introduce a magazine programme *This Morning*, into which daytime adult education programmes were incorporated. The ITC's adult education advisory committee expressed serious concern that there would be an inevitable trivialisation of content in 8-minute slots, and a narrowing of curriculum range. However, in the first winter of *This Morning* a series of six short programmes on New Opportunities for Women generated a huge response, almost all from women who had left education without formal qualifications. This success reinforces the point that well-targeted programming does reach and motivate people to participate, even in the daytime, but only for those people who are free to watch in the daytime. It is also fair to say that over the years *This Morning* has offered a narrower, more domesticated and less critical range of educational programmes than the free-standing series it replaced.

Channel 4 and back-up

Channel 4 has always shown a more consistently whole-hearted commitment to its education remit. Examples abound to show that television is capable of being used to reach target groups that education and training providers are least successful at recruiting, and stimulating them to take an interest in learning. However, as Naomi Sargant observes, it can also be a blunt medium:

> 'The disadvantage of broadcasting is that the message it sends is undifferentiated: everyone watching receives the same sound and picture irrespective of their needs and interests. . . So if the messages are to have the best effect, there have to be ways before or after the programmes for different individuals to relate to them and follow them up differently. This is the rationale for the development of a wide variety of readily accessible run-up, back-up and follow-up materials, using any medium which is helpful and appropriate.' (Sargant, 1992)

Since Channel 4 took the individual viewer as the learner or potential learner and a view that there were educational possibilities in the widest range of programming, it provided through Broadcasting Support Services a back-up capacity which could be used by programme makers across the Channel. The result was that Channel 4 consistently outperformed its legislative

remit to make 15 per cent of its programming educational, and it challenged the sharp distinction between educational and general output inherited from the BBC.

Although its audience was smaller that BBC1 or ITV, and its remit experimental, it succeeded in reaching beyond a middle class audience – not least because it adopted a programming strand aimed at employed people which it called 'for people with more time than money'. The consumer education programme *4 What It's Worth*, for example, reached more working class people than middle class people.

	4 What It's Worth	**Population**
	%	%
AB	13	15
C1	16	20
C2	32	35
DE	39	30

Figure 1: Profile of viewers of 4 What It's Worth, 1986 (Sargant 1992)

In its early years Channel 4 showed many of its educational series in the early evening, at 5.30pm or 6.30pm. Figure 2 compares the proportion of professional and middle class viewers (ABC1s) with those of working class viewers (C2DEs) watching a group of these series, the subjects of which ranged from DIY to architecture. (Sargant, 1992)

This pattern of response is strikingly different to the profile of participation in organised education and training mapped by NIACE's regular series of surveys, where ABC1s are consistently represented in greater proportions than their incidence in the population at large.

Social Action Broadcasting

The IBA required each ITV company to appoint a Community Education Officer (CEO). These staff played a key role in the educational mission of independent television companies in the 1980s. Their task was to develop a dialogue with the communities served by their regional service, to identify appropriate education and social action programming, and then organise appropriate off-air activities to complement it locally. They also worked together as a team to support nationally networked educational series.

For example, a short piece on conductive education in Hungary produced a flood of enquiries from parents in the Tyne Tees area seeking information on where comparable provision could be secured for children in Britain. Shiela Browne, the Tyne Tees TV CEO, organised a meeting on the issue attended by some hundreds of people, and a campaign followed to introduce conductive education in the North-East. Television can be a catalyst in the identification of needs. Properly supported, it can generate action.

Soap operas

There is no doubt, too, that soap operas can create a climate of understanding that makes receptivity to change more possible. The Archers was originally introduced as a vehicle for Ministry of Agriculture advice on changes in farming to be shared easily with a mass audience. Each major public information campaign is keen to persuade the soaps' production team to dramatise the dilemmas and challenges raised – from Aids to Cot Death to Adult Learners' Week, the evidence is that such exposure increases the impact of the campaign.

Ruth Hawthorn, in a stimulating piece for *Education Guidance News and Views*, describes

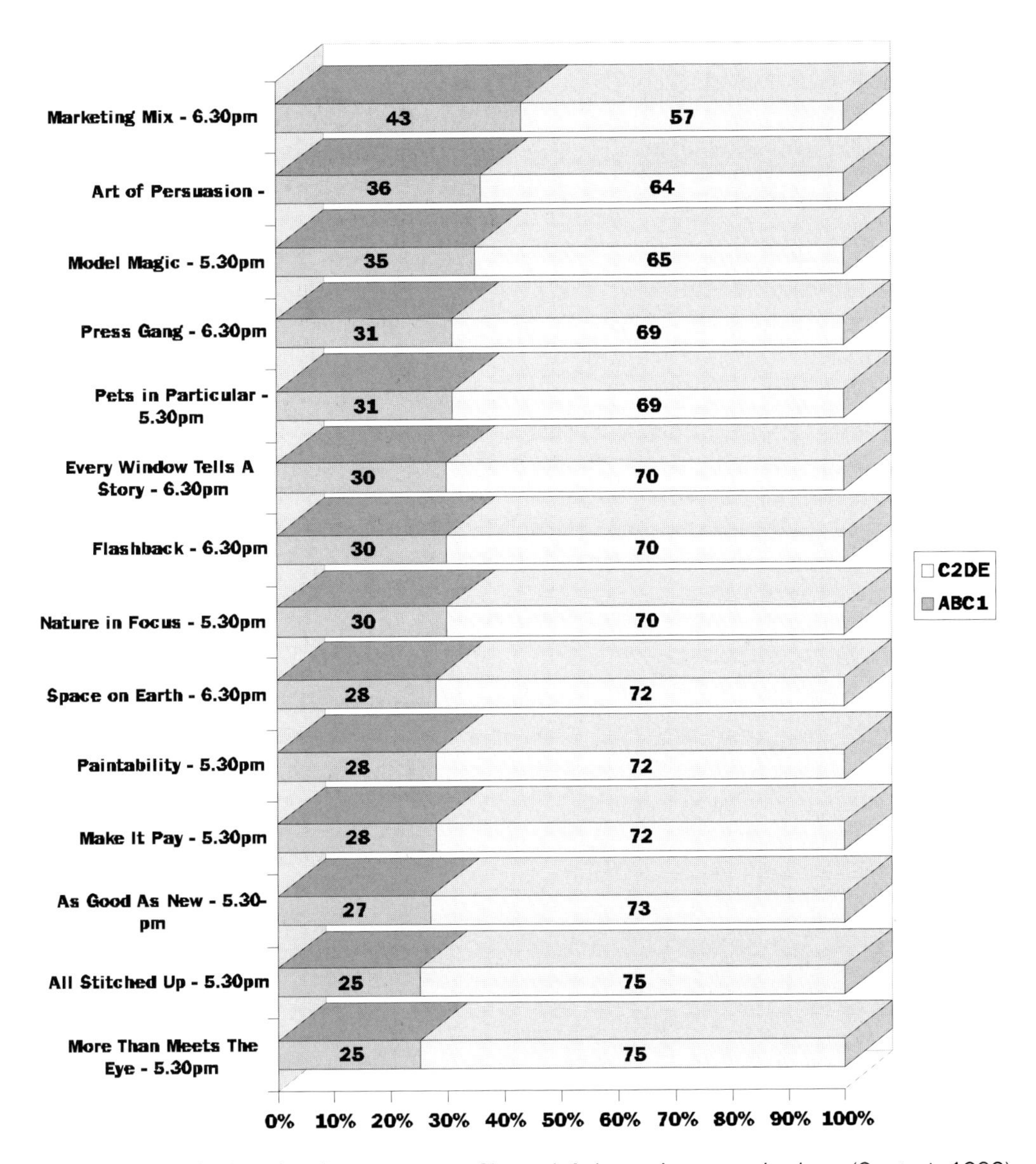

Figure 2: Viewers of educational programmes, Channel 4, by socio-economic class. (Sargant, 1992)

research into the way the media influence patterns of career choice:

> 'A young policeman told me how he had watched *The Bill* every Friday as a teenager, with his friends, at one or another of their houses. Several of his friends had talked about the possibility of becoming a policeman – one had even wanted to go into any uniformed job, but did not care if it was the army, the police or the fire brigade. My respondent thought this was ridiculous, because of what he saw as the opposite tasks of the police and the army. People see the different things in the same programme, even when the social context is the same for both of them . . . . . (T)elevision (and radio) can shape what we *do* at work. I asked if the work had turned out as expected. The policeman said *The Bill* hadn't prepared him for the long periods of boredom when he actually started work. But he described the contrast in his real life as a policeman between the long quiet boring periods and the

sudden need or action, decision, and strength. When action was required, he told me how his colleagues switched into being television policemen: they squared their shoulders and pulled in their stomachs and *acted* alert, as if the fiction had established the shared conventions about what it was to be a policeman in those moments.' (Hawthorn, 1997)

Family literacy

Soap operas are one illustration of the use of the different narrative forms available on the media. In the next section of the report there is an examination of the uses of different narrative forms in Adult Learners' Week. However, those weeks and the experience of the BBC/Basic Skills Agency Family Literacy Campaign show the power of guerrilla television. Since the introduction of advertising in the 1950s, viewers have developed a sophisticated understanding of cameo-length stories to sell goods and products. There was, in addition, a long tradition of public service announcements on independent television. London Weekend Television, in particular, developed these into short adverts, and were commissioned to make a memorable series of shorts on rights for Channel 4. Building on this in the Family Literacy Campaign, 1995, the BBC commissioned the advertising agency Bartle, Bogle and Hegarty to make three 90-second short narratives to encourage parents wanting to improve their own skills to help their children with reading and writing to call or write for a pack.

The adverts hit hard – bringing into play the anxiety and guilt parents feel when they don't think they can be of help to their children. This approach concerned the Basic Skills Agency before the programmes went out – at prime time, slotted between programmes with a mass appeal, since a key element of good basic skills work involves building confidence. However, 250,000 people asked for packs – wildly in excess of the anticipated demand to the delight of the Basic Skills Agency, who were put under great pressure, but successfully responded to the demand. People prompted to join in the Family Literacy pilot programmes introduced at the same time persevered with programmes of study (hardly anyone dropped out) and National Foundation for Educational Research's evaluation spoke in glowing terms of the effectiveness of the courses. Just as *On The Move* had contributed to the establishment of adult literacy provision nationally in the 1970s, these family literacy shorts have done much to reinforce the message that for basic skills intergenerational learning makes sense – the 'double-dealing dollar' as the American Tom Sticht calls it. (Sticht, 1991)

The Learning Zone

For many years the BBC's educational advisory committees reflected on the difficulties of serving further education colleges effectively. Schools broadcasting was well-established, and in specific areas of the curriculum (eg, in primary music) was well integrated into schools' work – at least until The National Curriculum came along. Programming for adults as independent learners was also well-developed – notably in languages education on the BBC and in health programming on ITV. However, the diversity and the fragmented nature of much of the further education sector made it hard to see what broadcasters could do direct.

It was this that prompted the BBC to discuss collaboration with the MSC/Training Agency in funding *Second Chance* in 1992, and prompted the BBC to introduce *The Training Hour* on Sundays. However, the success of shifting dedicated provision for FE to the night time – as a major element of *The Learning Zone* – has been dramatic. For learners who know what they want to learn, with access to a video recorder, and the skill and motivation to programme it, the broadcasting of programmes in the middle of the night is little inhibition. Backed by well-made adverts for the programme shown in prime-time, *The Learning Zone* has gained a greater audience consciousness of the availability of such programmes than for any previous initiative. In addition, *The Learning Zone* has shown that there is a significant, if small, number of viewers who watch the programmes direct.

Summer Nights

The success of *The Learning Zone*, and evidence that a general audience would use night-time series led in 1996 to the introduction of *Summer Nights* – literally a summer night-school of liberal education, with week-long series addressing, for example, music, dance, with reworked or re-shown programming previously dotted through the schedule. The programming was backed by a pilot scheme offering viewers the chance to seek accreditation for learning centred around the use of broadcasting mounted with the University of Middlesex and the National Open College Network. There are plans to extend such linkages with accreditation in a new daytime BBC slot, in recognition that the opportunity to get credit may itself act as a stimulus to participation.

Housebound Older Learners

For individual institutions, it can often feel as if television works on too broad a canvas for effective collaboration to be developed. However, the Putney Housebound Older Learners project developed in 1987 with the help of Channel 4 showed that such collaborations can work effectively. The project brought together class-based activity using a television series as a stimulus for study, paralleled by one-to-one tutorials for housebound learners, who followed the same programme of study. The tutorials were run by students attending the institute-based classes. Changes in funding have led to the project losing its budget after almost a decade – but its use of television programmes was imaginative and creative.

Deafness

Both the BBC and Channel 4 have proud records in programming for people who are deaf and hard of hearing – built around core programming (*See Hear*, BBC; *The Listening Eye* and *Same Difference*, Channel 4). Channel 4 with Tyne-Tees Television focused especially on people who are users of British Sign Language (BSL) and increasingly involved them in the production of programmes supporting a production training course run by the North East Media Training Centre. Channel 4's Deaf Day on 31 October 1990 signed or subtitled every programme on open screen. Presentation links and trailers were similarly captioned and signed. The centrepiece of the day was the British television premier of *Children of a Lesser God*. The day was designed to coincide with the centenary of the British Deaf Association, to raise awareness of the needs of deaf people. It was striking that there was no clear linkage, however, with education and training providers.

By 1995, when the BBC linked *See Hear* with Adult Learners' Week – two half-hour programmes were mounted, linked to the Week; a minicom line was opened, backed by the European Social Fund, and 4,000 fact sheets on educational opportunities for deaf and hard of hearing students were also distributed.

Mosaic and Birthrights

The BBC's five-year project MOSAIC provided resources for trainers tackling racism and equal opportunities issues in various work places from 1989. It was complemented by the *Birthrights*

series, introducing good black independent production companies to the screen. However, as Carol Haslam observed: 'The most fundamental point is that minority groups want to watch the same programmes as everyone else and yet they are not adequately represented in those programmes, or behind the scenes either. Broadcasters are becoming aware of this.'
(Haslam, 1991)

If broadcasters still have some way to go, so do many educational organisations.

Radio campaigns: Euroaction and National Radio

Whilst television is distinguished by its capacity to reach everyone, the radio audience is segmented. Television plays an effective role in capturing the attention of, and enthusing large numbers from, groups under-represented in further education through the programmes which reach a complete cross-section of the population, but importantly including under-represented groups. Radio offers the opportunity for more targeted campaigns. Through the 1990s BBC1, backed by an Employment Department free telephone helpline service and linked to similar initiatives in other EU states, has run week-long education campaigns on Radio 1 – targeting unemployed people, and in particular young unemployed people among that channel's young audience. The Campaign combined interviews and information led by the disc jockeys who interspersed the education and information material with the channel's usual blend of music and banter. Up to 15,000 people a week called the Euroaction helplines. That success led the BBC to establish telephone information lines to support each of its radio stations. The BBC Radio Helpline is operated from Glasgow by Broadcasting Support Services which takes around 7,000 calls a day following up everything from personal finance to living with tinnitus and, of course, education – notably when GCSE and A level advice is provided in the summer months.

Local radio campaigns

Individual colleges have wide experience of linking with local radio to promote courses. As early as 1977/78 BBC Radio Stoke linked with literacy providers to develop a range of programming for basic skills students wishing to develop a wider range of studies. John Brown, Principal of Bethnal Green Adult Education Institute in London, was attached for half a day a week to BBC Radio London to promote adult learning in the first half of the 1980s – appearing on air, and working alongside producers. Capital Radio in London sponsors the course guide *Floodlight* and runs annual promotions linking learning and employment in liaison with local providers; Three Counties Radio regularly links with TEC, LEA and college initiatives to promote learning, and to give listeners a taste of what is involved in taking a course. (ALA & LBA, 1997) Clearly, black and Asian radio stations offer an effective mechanism for targeting minority ethnic communities.

Cable

Croydon Community Education and Training Service, Croydon College and Sutton College of Liberal Arts have linked effectively with the local cable service provider for their daily local programming, and until its change of focus *The Learning Channel* – the dedicated cable learning channel – promoted participation in lifelong learning. Although cable's audience is small it is motivated: in 1993's Adult Learners' Week, for example, *The Learning Channel* received requests for 3,000 packs of support material, against 1,000 requests for Channel 4's offer, though the television programmes had reached perhaps ten times as many viewers. However, the very fact that dedicated channels reach already committed learners limits their usefulness in widening participation. This is a problem, too, facing further education in thinking how effectively to link with satellite programming. As Naomi Sargant's paper shows, the pace of change in the technologies and proliferation of channels may mean that one effective mechanism for promotion may be to put open learning materials onto the new satellite channels. (Sargant, 1992) The Open University still gets in excess of 2,000,000 people a week eavesdropping on its programming, and it may be that this route will be increasingly cost-effective for further education – if programme production and distribution costs can be contained.

The Press

All Further Education sector institutions recognise the value of the press as a mechanism for alerting local communities to the existence of courses, to the achievements of learners, and to the impact of colleges as major institutions in a community. Dennis MacShane's classic advice in *Using The Media* that you should say who, what, when, where, and why you want coverage in the first sentence, follow it with a quote and then text written so that it can be used verbatim by a busy journalist with space to fill, is understood by many marketing officers – at least in relation to the local press. (MacShane, 1979)

However, as a sector further education does less than others to promote itself in the myriad of weekly and monthly periodicals, the trade press, or in the nationals. All the specialist disability and minority ethnic press seem to carry more articles about schools and higher education than about further education. In part this may be the result of the pressure the sector is under, in part its diffidence. Too often further education is characterised as a sector in which knowledge, skills and values are transmitted rather than produced. However, it may be that marketing and promotion have been left too much to specialists. Few staff are trained and encouraged to write about the work for public audiences. FEFC could set an example by building on the work of its admirable information office with regular targeted briefings for media outlets for the minority ethnic community press, for women's magazines, and for a wider array of the national press.

It is important to recognise that managing bad news can be helpful, too. When I worked at Clapham-Battersea Adult Education Institute in ILEA a last-minute reorganisation of the numbering of Centres in the key to the map in the prospectus was not matched by a corresponding change in numbering on the map itself. Too late we realised we had produced 40,000 papers listing 1,500 courses not one of which would happen at the sites we advised people to go to. The Institute issued a press release 'Evening Class Chiefs Go To The Bottom Of The Class'; the *Evening Standard* carried it prominently, and we had our largest ever enrolment.

The argument throughout these examples is that is it possible to establish creative links between people working in the media and people working in education. Their interests are not exactly the same; their language and priorities differ. However, by learning enough of each others' needs it is possible to extend access to learning for very large numbers of people currently excluded. However, the media cannot wave a magic wand. As Ruth Hawthorn argues in respect of the influence of television on career choice:

> 'Television and radio among the people I interviewed had not been a source of new *ideas* for work but they did play a part in enlarging the understanding of some, once they had an idea for a job. . . The ideas for jobs usually come from one of those influential individuals at home (often an aunt or cousin) or from a subject teacher at school. If they were

> already interested, they would then seek out or pay more attention to programmes which touched on that interest.'

She concludes 'broadcast television has a powerful and valuable part to play in careers choice, and just as we are learning how it might be used, resources and time seem scarcer than ever.' (Hawthorn, 1997)

Adult Learners' Week

This section of the report looks at Adult Learners' Week, which seeks to bring the various strands of media providers, guidance workers and policy makers together to fire interest and widen participation.

Adult Learners' Week in Britain was adapted from a model developed without strong media links or telephone guidance in the USA. Its purpose is simple and straightforward – to celebrate existing adult learners in all their diversity in order to encourage others to participate. A distinctive feature of the Week in the UK has been the willingness of all four terrestrial television channels, cable and satellite television channels, BBC and commercial radio stations to collaborate in the Week each year. The Week is co-ordinated each year by NIACE – the National Organisation for Adult Learning, with major sponsorship from the European Social Fund, and from the Department for Employment and Education.

Key features of Adult Learners' Week

- Broadcasting on all terrestrial channels A free telephone helpline, staffed by guidance workers – attracting up to 57,000 callers, a third of whom take up courses as a result of the advice, and more than half of whom are long-term unemployed
- 5,000 local events
- Publicity for the helpline is distributed in every unemployment benefit pay cheque in the two weeks before the Week
- Regional outstanding adult learners' awards for individuals, chosen by cross-sectoral committees in each region
- National awards for outstanding groups of adult learners
- National awards for organisations fostering innovative programmes for adult learners
- A ministerial reception to launch the Week and to award the national prizes
- Regional award ceremonies for each ITV region
- A Parliamentary reception
- National policy conferences
- A press pack – producing national, regional and local press publicity, totalling 800 cuttings in 1996
- Local radio coverage
- A permissive structure – enabling anyone to identify with the Week
- National co-ordination by NIACE, including distribution of award details, newsletters, stimulus to undertake unusual events
- Funding from a variety of sources – the European Social Fund, the Department for Employment and Education, industrial, commercial and media sponsorship
- Exhibitions, carnivals of learning, 'Growing Old Disgracefully'
- Fun

National initiatives

Broadcasting: The BBC

The Evaluation Report of *Second Chance*, the BBC's contribution to the first Adult Learners' Week in 1992, noted: 'Although the BBC had had previous experience of orchestrating large campaigns (eg, *On The Move* and *A Way With Numbers*) such a high-profile, intensive and expensive week of bi-media broadcasting had not been tried before.' The BBC's television broadcasts that year consisted of fifteen light-hearted sketches, lasting approximately a minute and a half each, which were shown at peak times on BBC1 and featured top television personalities, and of five 15-minute documentaries shown in the late evening on BBC1. Each sketch highlighted a common anxiety about learning, the benefits to be gained, and ended with details of the Helpline. 1994's sketches show the range of issues covered:

Bankrupt: featured Nigel Havers and Dennis Waterman and particularly targeted men facing redundancy and unemployment.

Between The Lines: featured Neil Pearson and Siobhan Redmond with the message that language-learning brings personal benefits and that busy people can find the time to study.

Dracula – Prince of Darkness: featured Lesley Grantham and Sarah Crowe and targeted young women and non-traditional fields of training

Keeping Up Appearances: with Patricia Routledge and Josephine Tewson targeted older women who have been out of the workforce for some time.

Lovejoy: with Ian McShane and Dianne Parrish and targeted small employers, encouraging them to support their staff in gaining NVQs.

Wine Bar: featured Karl Howman and Roger Griffiths and targeted unemployed men and the work-based focus of NVQs.

The Brittas Empire: featured Chris Barrie, Michael Burns and Julie St. John and targeted men with few or no qualifications who feel stuck in present work.

2 point 4 Children: featured Belinda Lang and Gary Olsen and targeted people who might feel embarrassment about taking up learning for pleasure.

Casualty: featured Ian Bleasdale and Donna Croll, and targeted young, unskilled people and mentioned GNVQs.

EastEnders: featured Wendy Richard and Susan Tully and targeted busy but underemployed women with few or no qualifications.

Sketches were seen and remembered.

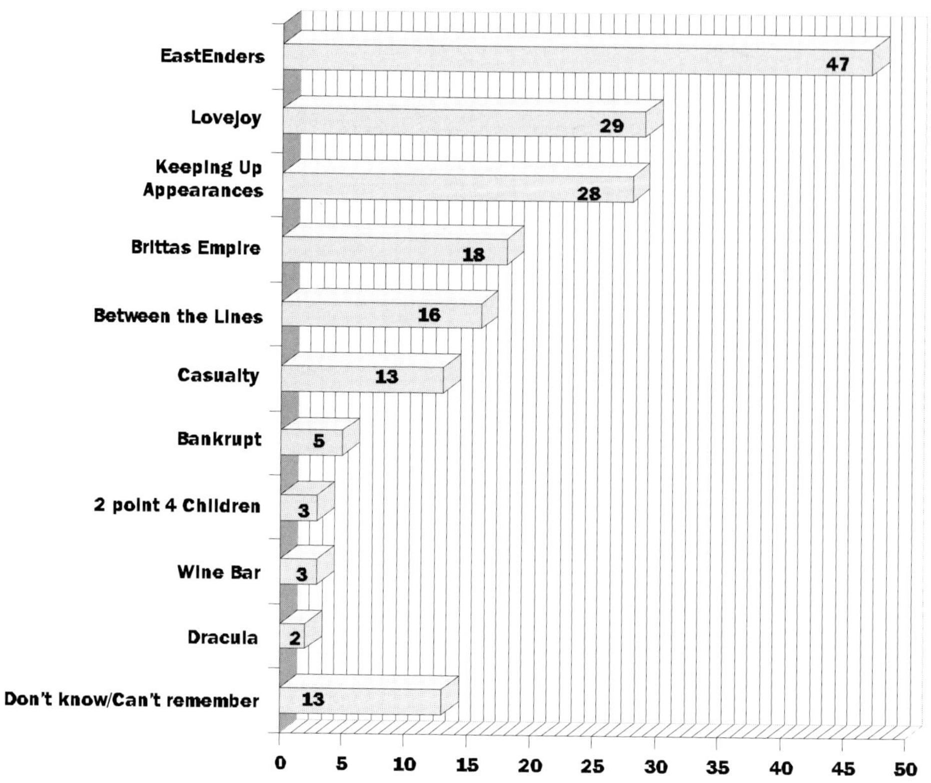

Figure 3: Awareness of Second Chance through sketches seen (Quigley, 1992)

In 1992 five documentaries included one on the country's only Access courses in nursing. Overwhelmed by the volume of demand from potential students many colleges introduced such courses in the following academic year. Radio coverage ranged from Charles Handy's *Thought for the Day* to *Woman's Hour* and *Education Matters* on Radio 4; promotion of the helpline number on Radio 1, and *Learn to Earn* on Radio 5.

A very detailed breakdown of the viewing pattern of the BBC programming was undertaken in 1994. It showed daily totals of *Second Chance* viewing of up to 25 million people, with more than 9 million watching one sketch.

Day	Daily Viewing Figures (millions)	Programme Duration
Sun 8	5.8m	36 mins
Mon 9	24.8m	7 mins
Tue 10	13.9m	3 mins
Wed 11	20.6m	10 mins
Thu 12	9.1m	1 min
Fri 13	24.2m	5 mins
Sat 14	15.3m	2 mins
Sun 15	12.7m	32 mins

Figure 4: BBC TV Daily Schedule (assumes new/different viewers of each Second Chance *transmission)* (Quigley, 1992)

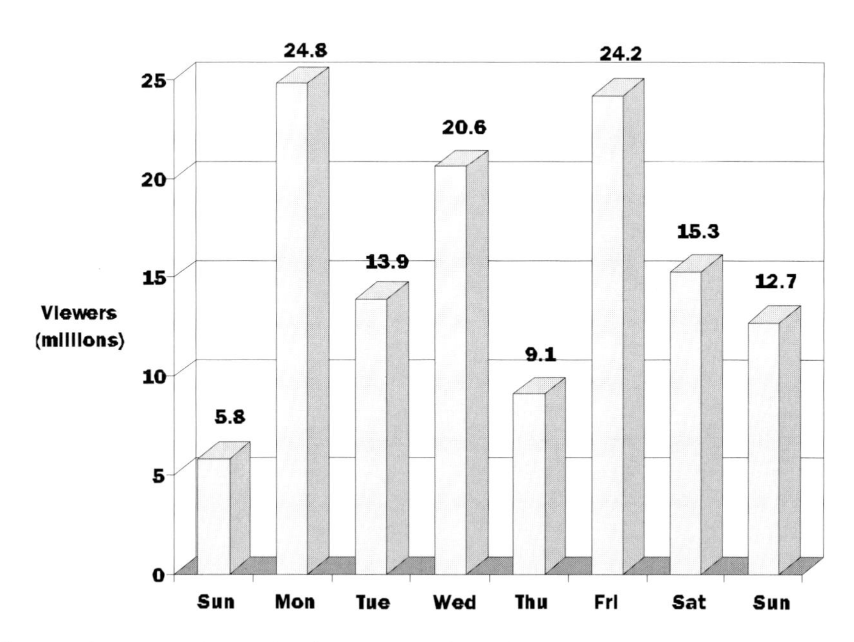

Figure 5: Second Chance *Daily viewing figures, May 8th–15th* (Quigley, 1992)

Time	Second Chance Programme	Duration	Average audience (millions)
Sunday 8 May			
11.00	Documentary 1	30 mins	0.2
14.50	Casualty Sketch	1 min	2.3
17.25	Documentary 'short' 1	5 mins	3.3
Monday 9 May			
12.15	East Enders Sketch	1 min	1.2
13.50	Bankrupt Sketch	1 min	3.8
17.35	East Enders Sketch	1 min	5.9
19.30	Keeping Up Appearances Sketch	1 min	3.8
21.00	Between The Lines Sketch	1 min	5.7
22.10	Documentary 'short' 2	5 mins	3.0
23.40	Dracula Sketch	1 min	1.4
Tuesday 10 May			
18.00	Keeping Up Appearances Sketch	1 min	5.9
22.00	Lovejoy Sketch	1 min	7.3
23.45	Wine Bar Sketch	1 min	0.7
Wednesday 11 May			
12.15	Dracula Sketch	1 min	0.9
13.30	Between The Lines Sketch	1 min	3.6
15.35	2point4 Children	1 min	1.1
20.00	The Brittas Empire Sketch	1 min	4.2
21.30	Lovejoy Sketch	1 min	6.9
22.25	Documentary 'short' 3	5 mins	3.9
Thursday 12 May*			
Four sketches withdrawn following news of the death of Labour Leader John Smith. Not re-scheduled.			
21.58	Between the Lines Sketch	1 min	9.1
Friday 13 May			
12.55	Bankrupt Sketch	1 min	2.4
15.00	Keeping Up Appearances Sketch	1 min	1.4
17.35	EastEnders Sketch	1 min	5.7
20.00	2point4 Children Sketch	1 min	5.1
Saturday 14 May			
18.00	The Brittas Empire Sketch	1 min	7.0
21.10	Bankrupt Sketch	1 min	8.3
15 May	SUNDAY		
11.00	Documentary 2	30 mins	0.3
17.30	Casualty Sketch	1 min	4.2
21.30	Keeping Up Appearances Sketch	1 min	6.2

Figure 6: Programme Schedules

Broadcasting: Independent Television

The impact of ITV has been national – though each company's contribution is regional in impact. The main focus of regional ITV activity in 1992 was, and remains, through Outstanding Adult Learners' Awards. These awards, for individuals and groups, are made by cross-sectoral regional planning bodies including representatives from colleges, TECs, the voluntary sector, adult education services, industry and television, to illustrate the strength and diversity of adult learners. Winners do have exceptional stories, but they are seen as emblematic of the experiences of adults in general. NIACE administers and co-ordinates the Awards process, and supports regional planning. ITV companies each make their own decisions abut how to be involved in the Week's activities. Characteristically, they show profiles of the region's winners, and/or the award ceremony, either on regional news programmes or in a dedicated slot. Community Service Announcements, teletext pages and continuity links promote the helpline.

Broadcasting: Channel 4

Channel 4's contributions have varied each year. In 1992 the Channel commissioned a one-and-a-half-hour drama *Homer and His Pigeons*, about an autodidact; in 1993 its opinion programmes following the news were all used for lifelong learning issues. They have had a series of films focusing on men returning to study, on IT and adult learning, and on mentorship.

The main broadcasts have all promoted the free telephone helpline, managed by the Employment Department Broadcasting Unit (DfEE following the amalgamation of the departments), which has operated from early morning – to catch enquirers stimulated by breakfast television, through to late evening. Mounting the helpline is a complex business.

Responses to the Helpline

As the 1994 BBC evaluation study reported, there were 51,414 calls to the helpline over the eight days *of Second Chance* broadcasting. Helpline centres were set up in Blackpool, Stirling, Cardiff, Bangor, and Belfast. Altogether, 66 incoming lines and 140 outgoing lines were available to take and return calls from all over the UK. Callers to the single 0800 100 900 freephone number were automatically routed to the appropriate helpline. Over 200 staff were recruited from local job centres to take calls and log details of the enquiries. 1,100 specialist advisers from guidance services, careers services, colleges, TECs and the Employment Service called back with specific, individual advice and gave local contacts for further information. Speakers of 20 minority and European languages were on hand, and specialist advisers were available to callers with disabilities or learning difficulties. Volunteer advisers from the Samaritans were also present.

From 1994 everyone claiming unemployment benefit has received details of the helpline and encouragement to ring the line with their payment cheque in the two weeks leading up to Adult Learners' Week. Research for NIACE has shown that recipients do not feel any coercion to ring, yet the impact has been dramatic. The flyer became in 1994 the largest single source of calls. It also had a dramatic impact on the profile of callers, with more than half of all callers registered unemployed.

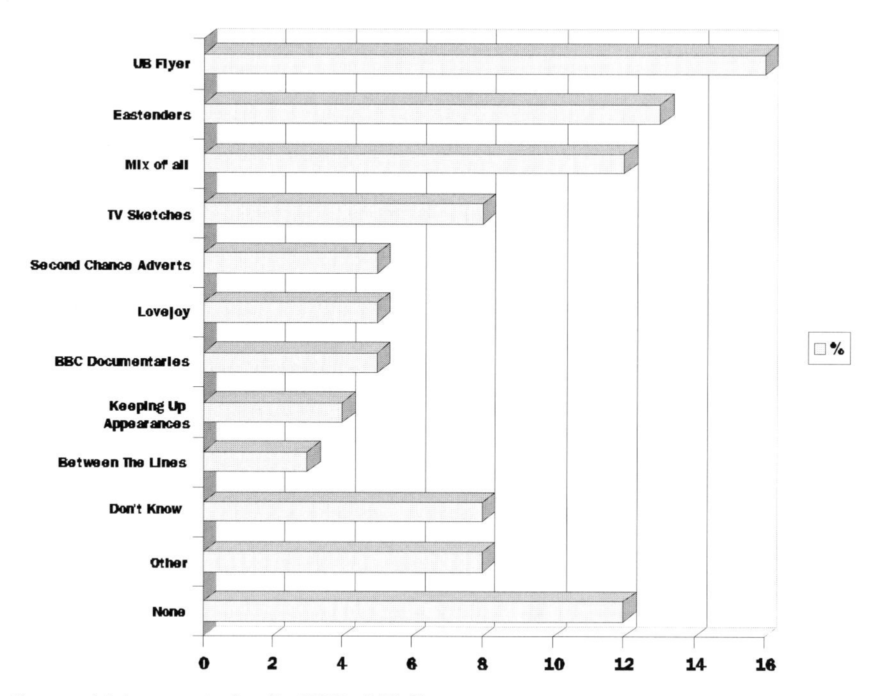

Figure 7: Items which prompted calls (BBC, 1994)

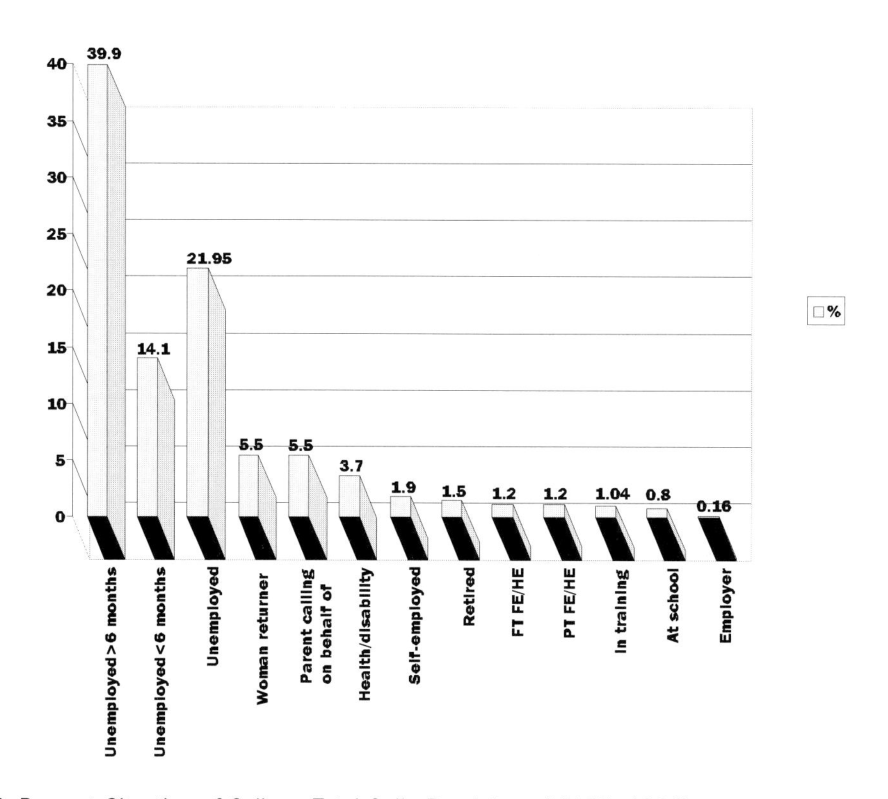

Figure 8: Present Situation of Callers: Total Calls Breakdown (NIACE, 1994)

These numbers are all the more dramatic when contrasted with research evidence of current levels of participation, and future intentions to participate, measured by NIACE's regular surveys, and by the BBC's Television Opinion Panel which show that participation relates strongly to social class, and that long-term unemployed people are significantly under-represented in learning activities. These surveys make clear that very few people who have not participated since school expect to do so in future. It is this that makes clear that the helpline response rates are impressive, and that television can trigger participation.

None since school	**NIACE/GALLUP 1996 sample)**	**BBC/TOP 1994 sample)**
	%	%
AB	19	21
C1	27	28
C2	42	42
DE	53	49
Overall	36	37

Figure 9: Who Participates? (Sargant, 1997)

Future Intentions				
	NIACE/GALLUP 1996		**BBC/TOP 1994**	
Likely to return	Not very	Not at all	Not very	Not at all
Non-returners	7	74	15	56
Overall	9	46	18	35

Figure 10: Future Intentions (Sargant, 1997)

The age profile of callers is again interesting – with a very even spread of callers for each ten year group between 20 and 50, and the interests expressed by callers demonstrate the relevance of the Week's initiatives to further education.

Bases 6,298 (15%) daily of 41,988 calls received					
Gender	%	**Status**	%	**Interest**	%
Male	54	> 6 mth Unemployed	39	Training/NVQs	24
Female	45	< 6 mth Unemployed	14	Further Education	23
		Employed	21	Info/advice/guidance	18
Age		Women Returners	5	Jobseeking	9
20–29	24	Parent	5	Grants	7
30–39	27	Disabled	3	Higher Education	7
40–49	23	Self Employed	1	Learning for Pleasure	2
50+	14	Retired	1	Self-employed	2
		F/T FHE	1	Basic skills/ESOL	1
		P/T FHE	1		
		Training	1		

Figure 11: Helpline Response Daily Analysis Blackpool 8–15th May (BBC, 1994)

A sample of callers are followed up each year to find out the lasting effectiveness of the helpline. In 1996, a survey of 500 callers to the helpline carried out for NIACE by ISR showed:

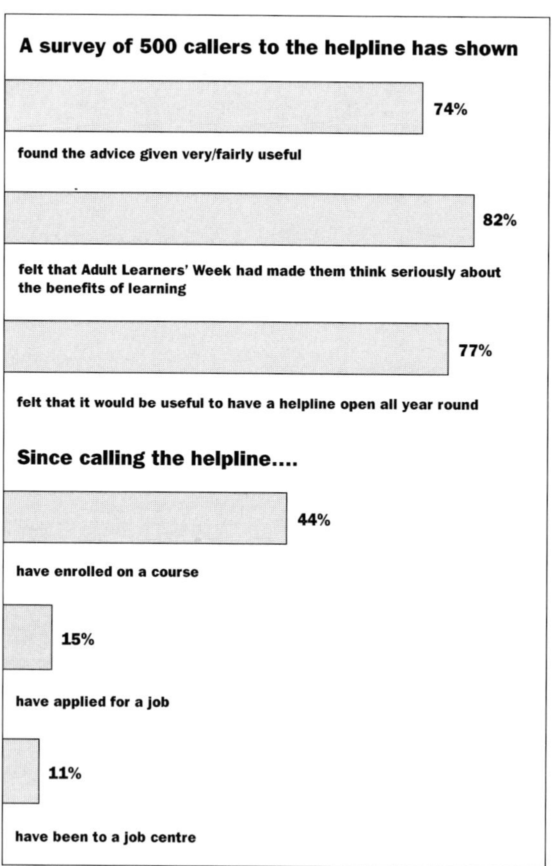

Figure 12: Survey of helpline callers (NIACE, 1996a)

Helpline advice is supported by an advice booklet published by the Department for Education and Employment, which is also distributed to libraries, job centres and colleges. In 1996 130,000 copies of *Free Your Potential*, a 72-page-booklet was circulated, and a tape version was distributed to blind and partially-sighted enquirers. (NIACE, 1996b)

National events

A key feature of the Week is that NIACE organises as little as possible in the centre, concentrates on widespread and early distribution of publicity material, and on the creation of a permissive and inclusive framework, within which organisations can set their own priorities. However, each year the Week does include a number of national events:

- A ministerial launch – to which all Award winners are invited, and at which group winners and organisations opening up access receive presentations, TV companies show extracts of their coverage, and politicians and celebrities speak.
- A national conference at IBM – highlighting adults' participation across all sectors of post-compulsory education and training.
- A Parliamentary reception – hosted by the All Party Parliamentary Group on Adult Education.
- A focus on adult learning in *Education Guardian*.
- Publication of newsworthy participation-related research is timed to coincide with the week.

Improving opportunities for adult learners depends on capturing and sustaining attention for adults' interests among the policy community – national and local politicians, administrators and institutional managers. This is a vital dimension of the role the Week plays in widening participation. The Week provides strong evidence for suggesting parties can in some contexts be a more effective tool in political persuasion than head-on confrontation.

A press pack is prepared and circulated to national, regional and local press and media outlets. This national intervention is designed to support and supplement regional and local contacts. Each year some 800 items are carried by the press, in addition to the welter of advertising undertaken by providers to coincide with the Week.

Adult Learners' Week is a UK activity. Television, radio and the helpline reach everyone. NIACE collaborates with partner organisations in Scotland and Northern Ireland, and co-ordinates a distinct range of activities in Wales – including the preparation of bilingual publicity materials.

Regional and local

However, as Tim Boswell, then Parliamentary Under-Secretary for Further and Higher Education observed in 1994:

> 'It would be quite wrong to think of the Week as predominantly a national event – though it is certainly that. Like adult learning itself, Adult Learners' Week is locally driven and locally managed. It depends on the creativity, imagination and hard work of thousands of people of all ages and backgrounds, throughout the country.' (Boswell, 1993)

A selection of the different initiatives mounted in 1995 captures the diversity of focus:

- Adult Learners' Radio – in a venture believed to be the first of its kind in the country, Adult Learners' Week was publicised in Bradford via its own radio station. The station, funded by Bradford and Ilkley Community College, took to the airwaves at 8am on Saturday 13th May and continued 24 hours a day throughout the week. Information and advice on learning opportunities was mixed with interviews with adult learners and celebrities.
- Two tickets to New York, donated by British Airways, was the prize offered by Cirencester College for a 'paper plane making competition'.
- In Gloucestershire, events organised by the County Council in collaboration with colleges, adult education centres and public and community organisations attracted nearly 2,500 people. During the week, staff and volunteers involved in adult learning and training went out into supermarket car parks and high streets to find out what opportunities people want for returning to education.
- The Vauxhall Motors Employee Guidelines Centre in Luton set up stands in the factory for the Open University, colleges, library and guidance services. A presentation ceremony was held on Friday 14th May for 140 employees who had finished courses in the last six months.
- The 'Ultimate Challenge' was devised by Hartlepool community worker Karen Milburn to promote Adult Learners' Week. She organised nine teams of adult learners from the Hartlepool area and challenged them to travel as far as possible in one day – delivering the 'learning for life' message along the way. National Express donated tickets for the teams – each team had leaflets about the Week to distribute during their travels.
- Bookmarks giving information about Adult Learners' Week events were inserted into every library book loaned in Oxfordshire.
- David Blunkett launched Adult Learners' Week in Yorkshire at Meadowhall Shopping Centre, on Sunday 14th May. The launch featured demonstrations, music, celebrity appearances and live interviews with adult learners. The event was filmed for Meadowhall Television and excerpts were broadcast at the Centre throughout the Week.

The Arts Council supports NIACE to encourage new patterns of provision in the Arts:

- In Birmingham the YES/NO Theatre Company performed a play about the experiences of learning as an adult.
- In Gloucestershire, Hesters Way Infant School and Family Centre opened its doors to parents and children for a week of arts activities. Headteacher, Sue Bride said, 'The school offers an enjoyable way back into education for many parents . . . a high proportion of parents are interested in the courses to improve their own understanding of their children's work.'
- 'Fire on the Water' was the theme for events in Chesterfield. A stall in the Market Place encouraged people to make lantern boats from beeswax, leaves and willow branches. A torchlight procession led the boats to their maiden voyage across the pond.
- Saltash in Cornwall staged its first ever Arts Festival with a week of free activities. Workshops included, watercolour painting, mobile making, textiles, lace, poetry reading, dance and folk music.

- Empty city centre shops were used in Coventry for free workshops in arts and crafts activities.
- Five adult education centres in Surrey were the base for painting sessions, an afternoon of poetry, prose, humour and dance.
- The Arabic Dance Group, Indian-jazz fusion and the Irish Folk Fiddlers were just a few of the performers to take to the stage outside the City Art Gallery in Leeds. Organiser Philippa Lester said, 'We want to promote a culture of adult learning . . . This will be a week to remember, to move people forward to learn something new'.
- In Lincolnshire, Stamford Arts Centre held comedy/drama workshops. It enabled women with no experience of drama to develop their dramatic and creative potential.
- The Working Men's College in London offered two days of free events ranging from art history, drawing, painting to karaoke and singing.
- In Liverpool, Mersey Ferries resounded with poetry, drama and music of all kinds in a boat load of learning.
- In Liverpool in 1996 provision targeted older learners with encouragement to try curriculum areas outside their day-to-day experience in its Growing Old Disgracefully programme.

In some regions, the regional dimension is limited to links with the television company and is organised around the Outstanding Adult Learners' Awards, with creative planning happening on a more local level. In others, supported by TEC and industrial sponsorship, a suite of regional activities are co-ordinated and promoted. The emergence of Gateshead's Metrocentre as a regional centre for adult learning guidance and advice in part derives from this. It was complemented in the North East in 1995 by among others a Learnathon organised by Newcastle WEA and Hartlepool's Ultimate Challenge. Given permission and encouragement to collaborate in what has been a very competitive climate, organisers let rip.

The experience developed in Adult Learners' Week spreads easily. Seedcorn funding from the European Year of Lifelong Learning provoked institutions to make the case for adult learning in fresh ways to new audiences in new settings. Among the EYLL initiatives were:

- A Pint and A Prospectus Please – Airedale and Wharfedale College linked with Tetley's to promote short courses in pubs.
- The University of the West of England and *The Big Issue* developed and then promoted provision for homeless people.
- Cut, Advice and Blow Dry – Rycotewood College took advice sessions to hairdressing salons.

The examples are legion. It is a strength of Adult Learners' Week that its goals are plural, and that it is owned by a great range of agencies. It is the permissive and inclusive structure of the Week that attracts sponsors offering support ranging from national posters to a local event. The pluralism, too, captures the complexity of adult motivation. Adults are notoriously untidy – seldom pursuing the purposes organisers had in mind for them.

Lessons

This paper has argued that through creative collaboration, organisers can think outside of their normal framework of reference to reach under-represented groups. The case has been made that there is an alliance of interest between people working in further education and those working in the media. Certainly, for under-represented groups innovative outreach strategies involving the media are critically useful in contesting prior experiences of failure – an attitude Veronica McGivney's study so aptly captures in *Education's for Other People*. (McGivney, 1990)

The case has also been made that television, in particular, has a powerful role in shaping attitudes – as the medium that reaches everyone it is clearly best-placed to play a role in widening participation, and in the creation of a society where we might reasonably have hopes of achieving the National Targets for Education and Training. Looked at from that perspective the decision of the government in 1990 to take away a statutory obligation to educate from Channel 3 licences must seem wholly regressive and unhelpful, as does the current remit of Channel 5. Surely, in order to maximise participation among the widest range of participant groups there is a need for *all* terrestrial broadcasting channels to be charged with a legal obligation to secure a range of educative programming. That obligation should be able to be met by promotional programming, of the kind so successfully pioneered during Adult Learners' Weeks. No state committed to the creation of a Learning Society can dodge its obligation to use any resources under its control to promote learning.

To achieve this would involve changes to the 1990 Broadcasting Act when ITV companies were spared any such obligation – but it is the first recommendation of this paper: **Government should consider the case for all terrestrial television channels (including Channels 3 and 5) to have a legislative duty to educate as well as to entertain and inform; and that that duty might be met through programming and support services that promote education as well as through directly educational programming.**

The case has also been made that motivation, and the stimulus to participation, is as much a curriculum issue as student induction, or course progression. Yet promotional initiatives are fragmented. Adult Learners' Week is successful – but every evaluation received makes the case for such initiatives at other times of the year. NIACE is considering a plan to complement the Week in May with a smaller-scale, poster-based initiative in September, *Sign On Now*, to increase the synergy available during the autumn recruitment period.

The second recommendation of this paper is that motivation and outreach work should be recognised as a central part of the further education curriculum. FEFC should consider the benefits of nationally funded and collaborative initiatives to stimulate participation – particularly from under-represented groups in January, May (to coincide with Adult Learners' Week) and September. It should consider a parallel initiative to Adult Learners' Week to promote participation among young people; particularly those who benefited least from initial education. It should also accept that funding for outreach work beyond funding to recruit for existing courses can be essential to widening participation to those groups least likely to join in by conventional means.

The case has also been made that the most effective promotional strategies combine national and more local initiatives. **The third recommendation of this paper is that the Committee consider as part of Widening Participation initiatives the case for funding a collaborative inter-agency initiative based on partnership with the media, in each of its regional areas for the promotion of widened participation.**

One of the experiences people working with adult learners share is that progress is made institution by institution, tutor by tutor. **The fourth recommendation is that each FEFC-funded institution should be required, as a condition of funding, within their strategic plan to identify priorities for widening participation, and the promotional strategies (including collaboration with other bodies at a local level) necessary to achieve widened participation.**

The argument developed in Naomi Sargant's parallel paper is that there is a compelling case that the media are not only good at stimulating demand, but are also good at meeting it – at least if the Open University's experience is adduced. (Sargant, 1992) **The fifth recommendation of these papers is that the case needs to be explored for some form of national further education open learning provision to complement local further education colleges as a strategy for widening participation.**

The sixth recommendation of this paper is for public funding to support and promote a culture of innovation and collaborative practice through an officially endorsed newsletter that highlights effective mechanisms for extending the learning community, and promotes the lessons of such innovation.

The final recommendation is that a library of visual images of further education work be developed to highlight the range of different people for whom it is a central experience.

References

ALA & LBA (1997) *Floodlight: the key to full-time courses in greater London 1997*. London: Floodlight.

BBC. (1994) Second Chance Evaluation. London: BBC

Boswell, T. (1993) The value and diversity of adult education. *Adults Learning* 4,10 265–268

Haslam, C. (1991) 'How we can develop a learning society?' in *Broadcasting and The Learning Society: a conference account*. London: BBC Education.

Hawthorn, R. (1997) Career choice: what part does television play? *Educational Guidance News & Views*. Callander: National Association for Educational Guidance for Adults (NAEGA), Spring.

HMSO. (1926) *Draft of Royal Charter for the incorporation of the British Broadcasting Corporation (Cmnd 2756)*. London: HMSO.

Hutton, W. (1991) 'The role of television and radio in the development of a learning society' in *Broadcasting and The Learning Society: a conference account*. London: BBC Education.

MacShane, D. (1979) *Using the media: how to deal with the press, television and radio*. London: Pluto Press.

McGivney, V. (1990) *Education's for other people: access to education for non-participant adults*. Leicester: NIACE.

NEC. (1983) *Make it count*. Cambridge: National Extension College.

NIACE. (1994) *Adult Learners' Week 1994: a report*. Leicester: NIACE.

NIACE. (1996a) *Adult Learners' Week 1–7 September 1996: a report*, Leicester: NIACE.

NIACE. (1996b) *Free your potential with Adult Learners' Week*. Leicester: NIACE.

Plowden, B. (1980) Shrinking employment: what role can broadcasting play in the next decade, Roscoe Lecture. 19 April 1980.

Quigley, K. (1992) *Second Chance Evaluation Report*. London: BBC Education.

Sargant, N. (1992) *Adult Learners, Broadcasting and Channel 4*. London: Channel 4 Television.

Sargant, N. (1997) *The learning divide: a study of participation in adult learning in the United Kingdom*. Leicester: NIACE.

Smith, K. & Malone, K. (1997) 'Seize the oars': guidance notes for organising Adult Learners' Week. Leicester: NIACE.

Sticht, T. (1991) Speaking at an Adult Literacy and Basic Skills Agency Conference, 1991

Also published by NIACE:

The learning divide
A study of participation in adult learning in the United Kingdom
Naomi Sargant with John Field, Hywel Francis, Tom Schuller and Alan Tuckett
ISBN 1 86201 016 1
144 pp, £20.00 inc p&p (UK)

The learning divide reports on a survey funded by the Department for Education and Employment, which was carried out for NIACE by the Gallup Organisation in early 1996. It highlights the full scale of the challenge which the UK faces in involving all its people in the learning society, and shows that the learning divide between the learning-rich and the learning-poor is growing.

Amongst its findings are the following: three in five of all adults have not taken part in adult learning in the last three years; more men than women are currently learning or have been recent learners; age is a barrier to participation; length of initial education is still the single best predictor of participation in adult learning.

The report includes the first full study of participation in Northern Ireland, and with national studies of Scotland and Wales, gives the most comprehensive coverage of the United Kingdom.

Lifelong learning in England and Wales
An overview and guide to issues arising from the European Year of Lifelong Learning
Alan Tuckett
ISBN 1 86201 012 9
40pp, £6.00 inc p&p (UK)

A report on the European Year of Lifelong Learning which looks at participation, learning goals and initiatives to encourage adult learning in the UK. An excellent introduction to the agencies and infrastructure involved in the provision of lifelong learning opportunities.

Adults Learning
ISSN 0955 2308
Published ten times a year

UK subscription rates: £40 institutions; £25 individuals; £15 part-time tutors and students. Multiple subscriptions: £15 each.

The need for a professional journal for those concerned with adult learning has never been greater. The majority of students in further and higher education in Britain are adults. More and more awareness of the importance of adults is being shown by government, the media, employers and trade unions. In a quickly-changing environment it is vital to keep abreast of current issues and initiatives, debates and events.

Adults learning is the only UK-wide journal solely devoted to matters concerning adult learning. It carries the latest news and views on policy and practice. It acts as a forum for adult educators and trainers to exchange information, share practice, network and engage in dialogue with fellow professionals.

A full publications catalogue is available from NIACE at:
21 De Montfort Street
Leicester LE1 7GE.
Alternatively, visit the NIACE website on the Internet at http://www.niace.org.uk